Poetics : East and West seems to me a major breakthrough in the arena of comparative theories. Much has been talked about western critical theories but Indian theories which anticipates some of the conceptual ideas of the western theories have been long ignored.

Sthitaprajna's book makes an insightful study on the ancient Indian theories and looks into the striking resemblance between the Indian and Western theories. This book becomes all the more relevant in the contemporary context because it initiates a possible interaction between India and the West. As she writes we can negotiate with the West better if we know our own theory well.

This book is certainly going to start a new tradition in not only Indian academic circles but also with scholars who have been trying to rediscover the Indian contribution to the critical tradition until now regarded as the monopoly of the West.

Dr. Umesh Patri

Literary Critic & Poet

It is fascinating to talk about theories but difficult to apply them to a text. The author tries to make the whole process of analysing texts more enriching by applying theories through Indian and Western parameters. Her attempt to see a possible interaction between the Indian and Western poetic theories can open new challenges for scholars and critics alike. Her attempt to build up a comprehensive theory taking into account the two critical traditions and justifiably applying to the texts is quite intellectually stimulating.

Michael Parker

Director

Arise Arjuna Foundation, USA

About the Author

Sthitaprajna is presently an Assistant Professor at the Institute of Technical Education and Research, SOA University, Bhubaneswar. She earned her doctoral degree in English literature from Maharaja Sayaji Rao University of Baroda, Vadodara.

Besides a collection of short stories for children, *Stories that Stir*, and books entitled *Parables of Jesus and Buddha: Exegesis and Anomaly,* as well as *Speak and Write Well,* Dr. Sthitaprajna has to her credit a good number of articles published in varions journals of repute in India and abroad. Presently she is doing her post-doctoral study on 'The Renaissance Philosophy of the 20th Century Indian and American Freethought Literature'.

Poetics: East and West

Sthitaprajna

Readworthy
New Delhi

First published 2010

Readworthy Publications (P) Ltd.

Editorial & Regd. Office	Branch Office
A-18, Mohan Garden	4735/22, Prakash Deep Building,
Near Nawada Metro Station	Ground Floor, Ansari Road, Daryaganj
New Delhi–110 059-06	New Delhi–110 002-02
Phone: 011-2537 1324	Phone: 011-43549197
Fax: +91-11-2537 1323	Fax: +91-11-23243060

Email: info@readworthypub.com
Web: www.readworthypub.com

Cataloging in Publication Data--DK
Courtesy: D.K. Agencies (P) Ltd. <docinfo@dkagencies.com>

Sthitaprajna, 1977-
Poetics : East and West / Sthitaprajna.
p. cm.
Includes bibliographical references (p.).
Includes index.

ISBN 13: 978-93-80302-04-1 ISBN 10: 93-80302-04-5

1. Poetics. 2. Sanskrit poetry--History and criticism. 3. Poetry--History and criticism. I. Title.

DDC 808.1 22

Printed at Salasar Imaging Systems, Delhi-35

On the Book Jacket

Poetics: East and West seems to me a major breakthrough in the arena of comparative theories. Much has been talked about Western critical theories but Indian theories which anticipate some of the conceptual ideas of the Western theories have been long ignored.

Sthitaprajna's book makes an insightful study on the ancient Indian theories and looks into the striking resemblance between the Indian and Western theories. This book becomes all the more relevant in the contemporary context because it initiates a possible interaction between India and the West. As she writes, we can negotiate with the West better if we know our own theory well.

This book is certainly going to start a new tradition in not only Indian academic circles but also with scholars who have been trying to rediscover the Indian contribution to the critical tradition until now regarded as the monopoly of the West.

Dr. Umesh Patri

Literary Critic & Poet

Preface

Few subjects have sparked more interest in Indian academic circles in recent years than post-modern literary theories. These ideas seemed particularly powerful in a self-consciously post-colonial society like India. Sthitaprajna's Poetics : East and West reflects the same continued interest in the legacy of Indian critical theories and poetic tradition in terms of its similarity in approach to some of the prominent Western literary theories.

Her specific interest in the Indian theories of Dhvani and Vakrokti and the Western School of New Criticism and Russian Formalism arises because of their shared ontological approach to poetic discourse. Moving beyond the ideological matrix, the Indian theories which are basically semiotic/semantic in nature have an almost similar interface with that of the Western theorists who grasp the imminent poetic form and its organic relation to society.

The author's argument that the Indian theory anticipates some of the conceptual ideals developed by the New Critics and the Russian Formalists could also spark a debate on the possibility of any mutual influences of the two poetic traditions. However, her convincing way of leaving out the Indian influence on Western poetics on grounds of antiquity creates a firm footing for the book in areas of academic and research interest.

It is fascinating to talk about theories but difficult to apply them to a text. The author tries to make the whole process of analysing texts more enriching by applying theories through Indian and Western parameters. Her attempt to see a possible interaction between the Indian and Western poetic theories can open new challenges for scholars and critics alike. Her attempt to build up a comprehensive theory taking into account the two critical traditions and justifiably applying to the texts is quite intellectually stimulating

Michael Parker
Director

Arise Arjuna Foundation
1620 N. 196th Place
Shoreline, Washington, USA 98133

Acknowledgements

I express my deep sense of gratitude to Prof. P. C. Kar, my teacher for putting me on the path with much valued knowledge and experience in the field.

My heartfelt gratitude to Dr Haladhar Panda for initiating the idea in my mind. I first became interested in Indian poetics when I got a chance to listen to him.

I owe a debt of gratitude to Dr Devabrata, a scholar on Indian philosophy and aesthetics, who spared his valuable time to discuss the subject at length with me and offered interesting interpretations.

My special thanks to the librarian of The M.S. University of Baroda and the staff of Bhandarkar Oriental Research Institute, Pune for facilitating me with my work.

Last but not the least, my parents who were throughout with me with their unflinching support and moral courage.

Sthitaprajna

Contents

1

Introduction

A literary work is a linguistic construct with a special use of language. This theoretical position is central to all the Indian schools of poetics and some Western critical thoughts as well. Literature takes a diametrically opposite position to that of a scientific discourse and this opposition springs mainly from the language of literary discourse. The chief concern of the literary theories of ancient India has been, therefore, to explain the difference between ordinary language and poetic language. In the Western critical tradition too, especially the New Critical tradition and Russian Formalism, the primary aim was to study the "text" as a verbal construct and to analyze its unique use of language.

In this book I am concerned with the concept of poetic language, its nature and definition as interpreted by two major theories of Sanskrit criticism: the Dhvani and the Vakrokti, and the Western School of New Criticism and Russian Formalism. I'm especially interested in these literary theories because of their unified ontological way of looking at a literary work and the greater affinities between their theoretical standpoint. I do not intend to discuss any mutual influence of the Indian and the Western theories, although there are similarities in approach between the two traditions. The antiquity of the Indian theories do not tempt me to highlight the impact and influence of Indian poetics on Western theories. My purpose is to study the Indian and the Western theories independently and see, wherever possible, the points of convergence between them.

The Indian school of poetics was developed as an independent and indigenous system of thought, and was subsequently enriched by Anandavardhana and Abhinavagupta, and codified by Mammata, Viswanâtha and Jagannâtha. Similarly, the Western tradition from Aristotle to the present time offers a continuity of concerns by constantly redefining the intricacies of a sustainable literary theory. Together the Indian and Western theories can work towards developing a consistent general theory of literature.

Russian Formalism and the New Criticism made the earliest attempt at giving literary theory an autonomous and distinct status. Putting literary studies on a firm and independent footing, they paved the way for other theoretical movements. With these two systematic approaches to literature, the chaos of critical studies of the earlier time gave way to a more systematic and scientific approach to literary studies. The study of literature was based on the genetic approach, i.e., the sources and genesis of a particular work. Literary studies were reduced to a secondary discipline as it was always seen in relation to history, sociology, philosophy and psychology. The Russian Formalists' attempt to create literary studies as an independent science of literature and define the nature of the object to be studied allowed for the specificity of literary studies.

In directing literary studies towards development as an independent science of literature, the Formalists refused to take literature as a vehicle or an instrument of psychological or social studies; instead they looked upon it as pure literature, which cannot be reduced to history or philosophy. To them, to study literature is not to look for a reflection of society or ideas in it, but to analyze its "literariness" which is the most distinguishing feature of literature. For them what constitutes and defines literature is its differential principle, i.e., literature is different from all other fields of study. According to them, literature is not sociology, or history or moral studies; it is a unique mode of discourse and has to be seen in its relation to language.

Literature, thus, operates as a unique genre making use of language in a special way which is different from the way the ordinary people use it in their everyday communication. The way in which the literary or poetic language works is through a technique called "defamiliarization," a term which is valorized by the Formalists. The poetic language defamiliarizes our usual modes of communication, thus refreshing our everyday experience. Viktor Shklovsky, the leader of the Formalist school, has given an example of how dance defamiliarizes our habitual activity of walking. He says, "A dance is a walk which is felt, even more accurately, it is a walk which is constructed to be felt.[1]" Similarly, art revives our perception of simple things in life that we fail to notice, even the poeticity of the language that we have been constantly using. Poetry makes ordinary language "strange," "difficult" and "oblique." It breaks the "habitualization" of the things by making them strange.

So the aim of literary studies, the Formalists claimed, was to analyze the difference between poetic and ordinary languages. The technique of defamiliarization helps bring out the distinction much more sharply and vividly. In this sense, then, the form rather than content should be the subject of analysis.

However, the technique of defamiliarization was not adequate enough in explaining the ineffectiveness of certain conventional forms and hence later developments in Formalism introduced the term "foregrounding" for the sake of greater effectiveness. Tynyanov's "foregrounding" is a concept which

---

1 Viktor Shklovsky, "On the connection between the devices of syuzhet construction and general stylistic devices," in *Russian Formalism*, ed. Stephen Bann and John E. Bolt (New York: Barnes and Noble, 1973), p.48.

is especially responsible for understanding the dominance of a particular element or structure in a text as against the other structures. It works with an assumption that some elements in a text form the background, where a particular element is foregrounded and is responsible for the defamiliarizing effect.

Roman Jakobson, the founder-member of the Prague Linguistic Circle, highlights the term "dominant": "The dominant may be defined as the focusing component of a work of art: it rules, determines and transforms the remaining components. It is the dominant which guarantees the integrity of the structure.... The dominant specifies the work."[2] A literary work, for Jakobson, is a verbal construction which has other non-literary functions. But what makes it "literary" is the aesthetic function which is dominant to the extent of transforming other linguistic functions to literary ones.

The terms "defamiliarization" and "dominant" are theoretically wide apart from one another. Where "defamiliarization" seeks to make strange the habitual factors thus making a difference, "dominant" inherently involves power relations, i.e. the aesthetic factor is automatically granted the power to rule over other linguistic factors. Jakobson's aesthetic factor as an imperialistic power to dominate everything non-literary was severely opposed by the Bakhtinian concept of literary dynamics. It seems viable to bring in Bakhtin here because of the relationship he shared with the Formalists. One can say that Bakhtin and the Formalists shared a complementary relationship. Nevertheless, they had something in common. For Bakhtin, the Formalist distinction between the practical and poetic languages is only part of the distinction between hundreds of discourses within a language system, which he termed "heteroglossia" or dialogism of social discourses. But both believed that in the literary discourse the

---

2 Roman Jakobson, *Language and Literature* (Cambridge, Mass.: Harvard UP, 1987), p. 41.

focus is on the message itself: to instruct about the nature of language it uses.

Though the New Criticism and Russian Formalism shared a similar concern with what literary studies should aim at, they differed in their theoretical frameworks. While the New Critics agreed with the Formalists on developing literary study as an independent discipline, making it more scientific, the New Critics, however, could not bring in the objectivity and rigour of Russian Formalists. The Formalists did not accept T. S. Eliot's views regarding the relation of art to life nor would they have shared I. A. Richards' views on experience or value and certainly they would never have subscribed to his preference for neuro-physiology or psychology as a means of making literary studies more scientific. The Formalists were far more radical than the New Critics in issues concerning the definition and objective of literary studies. Where the Formalists exclude the non-literary, the New Critics explore the different relations between life and art, which the Formalits see as mutual opposities.

The Formalists fundamentally differ from the New Critics on the issues of meaning and form. For the New Critics, art conveys a meaning and form is the means through which the meaning of literature is conveyed. But for the Formalists meaning or idea is part of the available material which enters into literature to be put to literary use by the functional devices of literature.

In spite of these disagreements, my desire for clubbing them together here is because of their common interest in working towards a definition of poetic language through making a distinction between practical and poetic languages. Both look at literature not as a means to an end but as an end in itself.

The New Criticism started with the works of I. A. Richards and T. S. Eliot and went on to include critics like John Crowe Ransom, Cleanth Brooks, Yvor Winters, Allen Tate, R. P. Warren, W. K. Wimsatt. This critical movement began in the thirties in England and continued in the forties and fifties in the United States to become one of the most influential critical schools in the academic circle. New Critical approaches may seem old-fashioned today, but its relevance could be felt in the contemporary critical practices dominated by deconstruction and other post-structuralist methods of reading based on the premise that a work is an autonomous object.

Richards' distinction between two functions of language —the symbolic/referential function and the emotive function —echoes the Formalistic distinction between practical and poetic languages. The symbolic function is the language of science which talks about the factual and verifiable objective world. But the emotive function of language evokes feelings. Richards goes on to say that a statement used for "the sake of the *reference,* true or false... is the *scientific* use of language."But the language used for the "sake of the effects in emotion and attitude produced by the reference it occasions is the *emotive* use of language."[3] Unlike the symbolic function, here the words do not refer to an object of the external world, rather they convey a desirable mental state or emotions. In this sense, he calls poetry a "pseudo statement," where factual verification does not occur but it brings about the reconciliation of our impulses. And herein lies the beauty of poetry. The difference between ordinary emotive experience and literary experience is that the latter has a greater level and higher degree of harmonizing diverse and often conflicting impulses. This function of poetry, which Richards terms as synaesthesis, organizes our impulses into total harmony.

Richards does not go on to define the nature of the poetic form in a Formalistic sense; his interest lies in the experience produced by reading a poem. By relating art to life, he insists on the empiricist and humanistic value of literature. The

3 A. Richards, *Principles of Literary Criticism* (London: Kegan Paul, 1924), p. 267.

seventeenth-eighteenth century empricist philosophy created a base for Richards' recourse to human experience and critical response to a poem in terms of psychological concepts. He explains the process of reading a poem and the experiences and effects produced by it through psychology. But he does not accept Kant's notion of a special aesthetic realm in the mind for aesthetic activity. He says that reading a poem is a heightened experience and does not need a separate mental space as such.

The later critics like Cleanth Brooks and others accepted Richards' concept of an equilibrium of contradictory forces but rejected his ideas on neurology and experience. Richards believed that human beings are a system of conscious or unconscious desires which are in conflict with each other. It is important, therefore, to organize these conflicting impulses in such a way that will reduce frustration and bring in a kind of harmony; the degree to which art or poetic experience harmonizes the conflicting impulses is exceptionally high. Moreover, he believed that the text is a vehicle for conveying the experience of the author to the reader. The reader must recreate within himself the mental condition of the author while reading the text. The emotive use of language of poetry is a vehicle for communicating the author's experience to the reader.

For Brooks, the language of poetry itself contains the reconciling factor, which should not be looked for elsewhere [reader's experience]. He was concerned with the "words on the page" or the "close-reading" of the text. So the text was read as an autonomous object governed by its formal features and structure. By "structure" Brooks meant that the meaning of a poem which is "coherence" largely consists in its capability of harmonizing opposite impulses. In his *The Well Wrought Urn* he says, "A poem is to be judged, not by the truth or falsity as such, of the idea which it incorporates, but rather by its character as drama—by its coherence, sensitivity, depth, richness and thought mindedness."[4] This coherence or balance can be achieved through "paradox" and "irony," the two terms he highlighted. "Paradox" is a technique used to bring about harmony in diversity, and "irony" designates the connotative meaning to a word in a poem. The words function in a context, and this contextual basis renders an altogether different meaning to a word. The multiple layers of meaning fail to reduce a poem into a paraphrase. "Irony" is a significant concept in this sense because it brings home an important message that any attempt to paraphrase a literary work is a heresy.

Brooks' concept of irony finds an elaboration in William Esthetic's *Seven Types of Ambiguity*. Ambiguity, like Brooks' paradox, should not be taken in its literal sense or conventional meaning we generally associate with the term. Ambiguity, for Empson, is "any verbal nuance, however slight, which gives room for alternative reactions to the same piece of language."[5] Empson, however, does not subscribe to any sort of a verbal play giving way to more than one meaning, like puns, to be considered as poetic. He goes on to say, "In so far as an ambiguity sustains intricacy, delicacy, or compression of thought..., it is to be respected.... It is not be respected in so far as it is due to weakness or thinness of thought...."[6]

Like Brooks, W. K. Wimsatt defines the characteristic feature of a poem through a term, "icon," derived from the American behaviourist psychologist C.W. Morris. In his *The Verbal Icon,* he argues that the language of poetry is different from the ordinary language not because it uses a different diction, but it involves a lot other things like metrical schemes, rhythm, figures of speech, the syntactic pattern, etc. The

4 Cleanth Brooks, The Well-Wrought Urn (New York: Harcourt, Brace and Co., 1947), p. 256.

5 William Empson, Seven Types of Ambiguity (London: Penguin Books, 1947), p. 1.

6 Empson 160.

"icon" is an all-encompassing term which takes into account the poem as a whole, from its phonetics to the syntactic and semantic levels. Any verbal structure of the poem is thus an iconic representation of the meaning; for example, a broken sequence of words is iconic of a disturbed mental state.

Ransom's distinction between "texture" and "structure," Blackmur's concept of "gesture" and Tate's analysis of "tension" together with Wimsatt's "icon" and Brooks' "paradox" and "irony" are attempts to define the distinguishing properties of poetry. Through these attempts, the New Critics formulated devices and techniques for the analysis of poetic language. While the Formalists' approach was on a purely linguistic level, the New Critics urged for a special cognitive role for poetry on an empiricist line. The New Critical notion of structure included only meaning and not all the different levels of the text. The New Critics were interested in the convergence within the text rather than the deviation from an external norm. So they were less attached to the ideas of difference and defamiliarization and other linguistic techniques to study literature. Literary criticism should be concerned with meaning or "cognitive structure." By "cognitive structure," Cleanth Brooks means the organisation of meaning in the text, i.e., reconciling the conflicting impulses.

II

A similar ontological tradition started long back in India. The Indian theorists, unlike their Western counterparts, never argued about the object of critical enquiry which they unanimously accepted as the literary work. They considered the literary work as a finished product ready to be analyzed without taking the trouble to find out what the author went through while writing the text. In analyzing the literary work, they maintained the distinction between ordinary and poetic languages and went on to examine what makes the latter so special and distinct.

The analogy of the literary work to a human, consisting of a body and a soul, was something fundamental to all the critical schools. And everyone accepted that the literal words on the page were the body; where they consistently differed was when they tried to define what constituted the "soul" of a poetic body. There were five major Indian schools of poetics, each proposing a particular doctrine of the "soul" of poetry. Of the five schools–alamkara (figuration), guna-riti (style), rasa-dhvani (suggestion), vakrokti (obliquity), aucitya (propriety)–I will deal with only two of them–the *rasa-dhvani* and *vakrokti*. *Rasa-dhvani* is the first successful attempt at satisfactorily incorporating the theory of *rasa* or the emotive element into the concept of *dhvani* (suggestion), thus bringing in semantics and emotive element into the sphere of criticism; *vakrokti* strikes a balance between arid formalism and evocatory aspects of literary studies, synthesizing them into one comprehensive theory. Both theories, moreover, have affinities with the two Western theories we have discussed, bringing them into a common aesthetic context to evolve a distinctive trend in critical theory.

The *Dhvani* school, founded by Anandavardhana, is one of the most influential schools in terms of the development of Sanskrit poetics, placing literary theory in an entirely new perspective. The formalistic schools before Anandavardhana were much worried about the embellishment of the external aspect of literature and considered the texts which do not possess figurative speech non-literary. Anandavardhana's *Dhvanyaloka* was a breakthrough in the sphere of literary criticism; it introduced the function of semantics and infused *rasa* (emotive element) into literary studies, the two areas which were neglected and overlooked in the past. Anandavardhana introduced a third function of the word, "suggestion" (vyañjana) alongside the two well-known ones, i.e., "denotation" (abhidha) and "connotation" (lakshana) and claimed that the suggestive function delineates a poetic discourse. Defining dhvani, he says, it is "that kind of poetry, wherein either the (conventional) meaning, or the (conventional) word, render themselves secondary and suggest the implied meaning, [this] is designated by the learned as dhvani or "suggestive poetry."[7] But not all suggestive language is poetry, says Anandavardhana; only the ones suggesting *rasa* (aesthetic emotion) are poetry. Again, he says, aesthetic emotion can never be stated because it fails to arouse any emotion. By simply uttering the words "love" or "compassion" we cannot feel "love," and so it has always to be suggested.

In India, poetics was never dissociated from philosophy, logic and grammar. While some prominent schools of philosophy like the Nyaya and Mimamsa denied the existence of suggestion because it could not be objectively studied, suggestion nevertheless had an enormous significance for poeticians and linguists. The suggestive function of language defines and shapes large areas of our cognitive and emotive understandings as well as the socio-cultural aspects of our speech-act.

Anandavardhana's dhvani theory was influenced by Bhartṛhari, the ancient Indian grammarian. The name "dhvani" is also taken from the terminology of grammar which means "sound." Bhartṛhari's *sphota* theory was a precursor to the dhvani theory.

Apart from *Dhvanyaloka,* Abhinavagupta's commentary on it is an equally significant work on the dhvani theory. Abhinavagupta's insightful analysis, careful observations and keen sense of going beyond the mere literal text converts his commentary into almost another treatise on dhvani.

Unlike the dhvani theory, Kuntaka's theory of "vakrokti" did not postulate an altogether new concept. Kuntaka tried to synthesize all the existing theories and came forward with his

7 Anandavardhana, *Dhvanyaloka, trans.* K. Krishnamoorthy (Dharwar: Karnataka University, 1974), p. 9.

own called "vakrokti." The characteristic feature of all poetic language is "vakrokti" or imaginative expression, according to Kuntaka, and there are numerous forms of creating vakrokti. But again not all kinds of vakrokti are poetic; only those which have poetic charm or delight and are enjoyable can be categorized as vakrokti.

Though Kuntaka accommodates the theory of figuration and style into his poetics, his theory is different from that of Bhamaha's "figuration" or Dandin's "style." While Bhamaha's theory does not take into account any other aspect of the poetic discourse like the semantic or the evocative except figuration, Kuntaka's is concerned with form, sense and the evocative element. Kuntaka is not very keen on semantics alone like Anandavardhana but he accepts the principle of *rasa*. Although his focus is on imaginative expression, he could not deny the existence of aesthetic emotion because by then the notion of aesthetic emotion was put into a firm footing in literary studies. He felt that its exclusion from poetic theory would make the position of the critics weak.

In a literary work anything from a phoneme to a paragraph or even the whole text can be charming because of vakrokti, and this leads to poetic delight which ultimately evokes *rasa* (aesthetic emotion). Kuntaka treats in detail how letters, words, and sentences can achieve poetic charm in the light of other literary work. In his formalistic approach he is closer to the Russian Formalists.

Russian Formalism and the New Criticism are the two most widely debated theories. Many Western critics have used and abused these theories. Contemporary critical theories like structuralism and post-structuralism have challenged New Criticism's premises and assumptions by using some of New Criticism's own strategies. But some recent critics like Murray Krieger, Hazard Adams and M. H. Abrams have revived interest in it.

Similarly, a lot of pioneering work has been done on Indian aesthetics by both Indian and Western Sanskrit scholars. K. Krishnamoorthy, P.V. Kane, Krishna Rayan, Sushil Kumar De, K.C. Pandey, V. Raghavan, M. Hiriyanna, A. B. Keith, Daniel Ingalls, R. Knoli and J.L. Masson, to name a few, have contributed substantially to the debates about Indian aesthetics. V.K. Chari's *Sanskrit Criticism* is an excellent exposition of the major critical concepts of Sanskrit criticism from the standpoint of *rasa*. Critics like C.D. Narasimhaiah have constantly pursued a comparative study of Indian and Western poetics. Narasimhaiah's edited work *East West Poetics at Work,* a collection of seminar papers, is an endeavour towards initiating a dialogue with the West. K. Kunjunni Raja's *Indian Theories of Meaning* provides a groundwork for defining the concept of "meaning" in different Indian aesthetic and philosophical traditions having parallel with those in the West. Rama Nair's book *Theory of Language in Indian Aesthetics: A Comparative Approach* examines the Indian aesthetic theories in their totality, while discussing some Western concepts. But a comparative study of the two Indian theories I have studied here with the two in the West has not yet been done. So I take off from where others have left and propose to study the Indian schools of dhvani and vakrokti in a comparative way by taking into account the Formalist and New Critical Schools. I also intend to make a close study of each of the four schools to point out how each has evolved its own theoretical positions and interpretive strategies.

III

In exploring the different dimensions of language, philosophers, literary critics and linguists in India and the West have addressed the problem of meaning. Interpretation was something rudimentary to all of them, and the literary theorists largely depended on philosophical exegesis for the problems of semantics.

The study of semantics has had a long ancestry in India with most of the schools of philosophy working out different theories of meaning. Studying the function of language was important for most of these schools because they were involved in interpreting the Vedic texts. The function of language is to convey meaning; different types of meanings conveyed by speech are denotation (*abhidha*), indication (*lakshana*), suggestion (*vyañjana*), and implied meaning (*tatparya*) as highlighted by various schools.

The Mimamsa and Nyaya are two important schools which have made significant contributions towards linguistic study. Though both the philosophical thoughts took the word to be the minimum meaningful unit of language, they differed regarding the nature of the relation of the meaning with the word. The Mimamsakas believed that the relationship is a natural one whereas the Naiyayikas believed it as conventional. The Mimamsakas argued that the denotative power is natural and inherent in words and the relationship between the word and meaning is impersonal, i.e., it cannot be traced to any human being. The Naiyayikas, however, differ from the Mimamsakas by calling the relationship as conventional.

The Buddhists also accept a causal relation between a word and our mental construct of the image. Where they tend to disagree with the Mimamsakas is that there can be no real connection between a word and the object as we acquire the meaning with the construction of a mental image of the real object through a process of negation. For instance, the word "tree" does not actually define something with huge trunks and branches and leaves; it brings in the image of a tree by excluding all that is not a tree. This Buddhist theory called *apoha* comes quite close to Saussure's theory that the meanings of words are "relational." The differences and binary oppositions to other words define the meaning of a word. That meaning is always attributed to the human mind and the relation between the word and its meaning is arbitrary are aspects common to both Saussure and *apoha* theory of the Buddhists.

The arbitrariness of the sign that Saussure proclaimed suggests a functional relationship between the signifier and the signified rather than a direct one which, in turn, resolves to identify how we make sense of reality and not what reality is. In that sense, language no longer communicates experiences and is not a reflection of the world and reality but a system enclosed in itself. Like Saussure, Roland Barthes and Levi-Strauss have developed the notion that language is the only reality given to humans constituting their world. Literature, therefore, also does not express or imitate "reality" and works as a system with the same underlying principle as does other human discourses like myths, tribal rituals or fashions. Unlike the older literary criticism, structuralism's job was not to provide another interpretation of the text but to demonstrate the underlying structured set of signs or codes which governs the meanings of the literary text. So the structuralist critics' aim, as Jonathan Culler puts it, is "to construct a poetics which stands to literature as linguistics stands to language."[8]

Instead of the traditional practice of interpretation involving the author or context, structuralism allows a complete focus on language. In this attention to language we can see some similarities between the New Criticism and Structuralism, but their methodologies of studying this language is quite different. For the New Criticism studying language is a means to getting into the meaning; for structuralism language itself becomes its sole justification. As Barthes remarks, "The rules of literary language do not concern the confirmity of this language to reality (whatever the claims of the realistic schools), but only its submission to the system of signs the author has

8 Jonathan Culler, *Structuralist Poetics* (London: Routledge and Kegan Paul, 1975), p. 257.

established....''[9] He goes on to say, "The author and the work are only a point of departure for an analysis whose horizon is language," and continues, "we cannot have a science of Dante, of Shakespeare or of Racine, but only a science of discourse."[10]

Barthes' and Foucault's attack on the notion of the author, especially Barthes' aggressive announcement of the death of the author, is a reverberation of Nietzsche's skeptical statement that God is dead. By decentering the author, Barthes and Foucault do not completely dispose off the author. But unlike Gadamer they would not like to believe the author to be the source of meaning. Gadamer tries to bring in a "fusion" between the author and the reader in these words:

> *If we examine the situation more clearly, however, we find that meanings cannot be understood in an arbitrary way. Just as we cannot continually misunderstand the use of a word without its affecting the meaning of the whole, so we cannot hold blindly to our own foremeaning of the thing if we would understand the meaning of another. ...All that is asked is that we remain open to the meaning of the other person or of the text. But this openness always includes our placing the other meaning in relation with whole of our own meanings or ourselves in relation to it ... And if a person fails to hear what the other person is really saying, he will not be able to place correctly what he has misunderstood within the range of his own various expectations of meaning.*[11]

In negating meaning the Structuralists and Post-Structuralists denied the mimetic function of literature. Structuralism's assertion that language has no relationship

---

9 Roland Barthes, "What is Criticism?" in *Critical Essays*, trans. Richard Howard (Evanston: Northwestern UP, 1972), p. 258.

10 Roland Barthes, "Science of Literature," in *Structuralism and Literary Criticism*, ed. H.S. Gill (Delhi: Bahri Publications, 1979), p. 15.

11 Hans-Georg Gadamer, *Truth and Method* (New York: Crossroad, 1982) 238.

to reality is taken forward by deconstructionists' assertion of the uncertainties within the system of language. Derrida situates the text in the absence of the author, in the endless free play of meanings. We are sent to a gravity-free universe where the centre and the margins are "deconstructed" and there is no intellectual reference point. Geoffrey Hartman, in his introduction to the anthology, *Deconstruction and Criticism* writes, "Deconstruction refuses to identify the force of literature with any concept of embodied meaning and shows how deeply such logocentric and incarnationist perspectives have influenced the way we think about art."[12]

Language, for the Post-Structuralist, is considered fluid. Words are constantly floating and hence their meanings cannot be captured as fixed and permanent. Meanings, therefore, cannot be "planted," they can only be "disseminated." The stable meaning of the text gives way to a radical freeplay of meanings. The deconstructionist reading is, in this way, opposite to the New Critical reading—the New Critics see a kind of harmony or unity beneath the apparent disunity while the deconstructionists find the internal disunity, fissures and conflict in an apparently "safe-looking" text. So we have texuality instead of the text.

Derrida's attack on the whole of Western metaphysics from Plato to Rousseau is precisely based on his contention that the Western metaphysics makes the mistake of identifying language with *logos* or spoken word where writing is considered only secondary to speech. The Indian philosophers are also guilty of making the same point—speech is more important than writing. And like Derrida, Bhartṛhari, the Indian philosopher and propounder of the *sphota* theory, critiques the Indian metaphysical position of logocentrism.

---

12 Geoffrey Hartman, ed. *Deconstruction and Criticism* (New York: The Seabury Press, 1979), p. vii.

Reversing the hierarchical opposition of speech versus writing, Derrida follows Nagarjuna, the Indian philosopher, Nietzsche and Heidegger to expose the weakness of the Western position by applying its own strategies against itself. Writing, for Derrida, is not the mere inscription of words; it is the neuronal traces of the brain which is the creative force of all languages which Freud terms as "memory."[13] He, thus, states: "Language is not merely a sort of writing 'but' a possibility founded on the general possibility of writing." [14]

Bhartṛhari's *sabdatattva* or the word-principle is similar to Derrida's "trace" or arche-writing. The word-principle is responsible for all the speech and writing; there is nothing beyond it, says Bhartṛhari, which is echoed in Derrida's arche writing. Language does not depend on God, logos or Brahman; rather it creates all these—the word-principle creates the universe. Bhartṛhari and Derrida both believe that the intrinsic différance in the *sabdatattva* or arche-writing is responsible for the articulation of language as speech and writing. This can be distinguished as three forms: sign/*sphota* –the whole, signified/artha–the concept or meaning, and the signifier/*dhvani*–the uttered or heard sound.[15]

It is the *sphota* which makes understanding possible. According to Bhartṛhari's *sphota* theory, as discussed in his work Vakyapadiya, the parts are subordinate to the whole. We do not make sense of a sentence by joining its parts, i.e., the individual sounds and words; rather the sentence is grasped together as a whole. The two principles of the *sphota* theory are: a sentence is taken as a single, undivided utterance; its

---

13 Jacques Derida, *Writing and Difference* (Chicago: University of Chicago Press, 1978), p. 222.

14 Jacques Derrida, Of *Grammatology*. trans. Gayatri Chakravorty Spivak (Baltimore: The Johns Hopkins UP, 1976), p. 52.

15 Harold G Coward, "Speech Versus Writing in Derrida and Bhartrhari," *Philosophy East and West* XLI.2 (April:1991): pp 144-46.

meaning is evoked as a flash of illumination (*pratibha* or *sphota*). The sentence is considered as the fundamental linguistic and semantic unit and cannot be divided into phonemes or morphemes. Unlike Mimamsakas and Naiyayikas, the *sphota* theory does not study language from a part-whole approach, it argues for a whole-part approach like the Gestalt theory. We first make sense of the sentence and then go on to analyze its components.

But Gadamer and Wittgenstein together take different views. To them language is a "living" thing and one has to return to speech to know its authentic condition. Speaking a language, according to them, highlights the "doing" aspect of it and speaking involves participating in a "form of life." That is why, both insisted that language was full of games.

The later Wittgenstein of *Philosophical Investigations* replaces his concept of language as a logical system with the concept of language-games. Like games, languages are informal, plural and diverse and cannot be reduced to an underlying logical form. Language, moreover, cannot be confined to a boundary and lacks a foundation. The rules and meanings are agreed on the arbitrations of conventions and consensus. Language, like game, is learned partly through imitating and partly through rules, and one can never control language.

The notion of "play" and "game" resurfaces in Gadamer's *Truth and Method*. Gadamer is more interested in the distinction of the poetic and everyday language unlike Wittgenstein whose silence on poetic language reveals his positivistic philosophical allegiance. In poetic language, the words take on a life of their own, their "corporeality" is highlighted, while in the ordinary language the words lose their autonomy and vanish after the message is made. Ordinary language is, in the Heideggerian term, the language of the "homeland" and comes to life in the poetic utterance. Language is originally poetic, according to Heidegger, and we make a categorical mistake when we say that the opposite of poetry is prose. Prose can be equally poetic. Poeticity of language is lost through its constant use for everyday communicative purpose. Heidegger's metaphysical views on language have some parallels with some Indian concepts. However, I will limit my study to the parallels between Dhvani and Vakrokti theories and the Russian Formalism and New Criticism involving the nature of poetic language and, as far as possible, connect them to some contemporary theoretical perceptions.

2

Anandavardhana's *Dhvanyaloka*

Dhvani as Poetic Language

The Indian theory of poetic suggestion, developed and formulated by Anandavardhana in his classic work *Dhvanyaloka*, has surprising parallels with that of the West. The concept of dhvani, which could be translated in English as suggestion, is a term derived from linguistics and means sound. The sound in its final verdict suggests the phonological structure or identity of the word. Dhvani as poetic suggestion similarly justifies and establishes a third potency of language called vyañjana (suggestion), which accounts for the principle of the highest kind of poetry. For this the dhvani critics had to fight a long philosophical battle with the logicians and the philosophers, especially the Mimamsakas and Naiyayikas, who believed that language had only two functions of meaning–the primary (abhidha) and secondary (laksana). Dhvani theory has a wider efficacy because it could account for both the figurative and non-figurative aspects in poetry.

Although the Indian theory of dhvani and its Western counterpart have been developed at different times under different circumstances, there are many similarities between the 9th century and the 19th century formulations of the theory of suggestion as poetic language. Though the Indian theory of suggestion was an extension of the philosophical theorizing of language practised by grammarians, philosophers, and logicians and was basically a semantic theory having none of the mystical overtones of its Western counterpart developed under the influence of Blake, Coleridge, Poe, Mallarmé and Yeats. It was similar to its Western counterpart in propounding that the essence of poetic language lies in suggestion working at multiple levels of meaning. Both the theories had adopted different methodologies but nevertheless showed that emotion in poetry is essentially suggestive. The dhvani theroists lacked the notion of the "symbol," which is actually the foundation of the symbolist movement in the West.

Anandavardhana lived during the time of King Avantivarman in the later part of the ninth century. A Kashmiri, and a poet, he was aware of the tradition of literary criticism that had originated in Kashmir during the reign of Jayapida in the later half of the eighth century. The grammarian Ksiraswamin, the poets Damodara and Manoratha, the rhetorician Vamana and the critic-poet Udbhata were among the prominent members who graced the court of Jayapida. Udbhata was appointed as the chief of the court, which was more an academic body than a political one. This academy of poets and intellectuals had access to the rich library of Sanskrit and Prakrit classical works. They were aware of the works of the rhetoricians like Bhamaha and Dandin and of Bharata's *Natyasastra*. But not before Udbhata did anyone take up Bharata's *Natyasastra* as an important work that could shape the direction of poetics. The early poeticians Bhamaha and Dandin defined alamkara (figures of speech) and guna (qualities)-riti (style) as the soul of poetry, respectively. Though they were aware of rasa, they had not given due importance to it and mentioned it as just any other figure of speech.

It was Udbhata who brought *Natyasastra,* the ancient manual on dramaturgy, into the sphere of general poetics. He had written a commentary on *Natyasastra,* which might have inspired the commentaries of Lollata, Sankuka and Abhinavagupta. These commentaries were significant in establishing rasa as the bedrock of the poetic tradition. Ingalls comments:

> *The importance of this new interest is inestimable, for as we shall see, it was by bringing Bharata's doctrine of the rasas, the flavors or moods of a theatrical piece, into a general theory of literature that Ananda arrived at a critique which finally could furnish workable criteria of literary excellence.*[16]

It is unlikely that Udbhata was unaware of the term "dhvani" or its semantic function as the term "dhvani" was used by Manoratha, a contemporary of Udbhata. Perhaps, Udbhata deliberately leaves it untouched, according to Pratihara Induraja, his commentator, to work on the older extants. But the two important aspects of the Indian poetic tradition "rasa" and "dhvani," which were left to be developed later by Anandavardhana into a full-fledged system, had their origin in Udbhata.

Anandavardhana established suggestion (dhvani) as the soul of poetry ("Kavyasyatma dhvanih,") which can be said to be an extension of the rasa theory. The object of a dramatic art is the realization of rasa, according to Bharata. Anandavardhana also qualifies rasa as the object of any art, but rasa, according to him, can never be stated but be always suggested and it is only the suggested emotion which is charming and enhances the aesthetic value of a work of art. He declares:

> *Our effort has all along been to make it clear that the poets do well to have the sole intention of infusing suggested sentiments, etc. into their works, and not merely to exhibit our enthusiasm in propounding a novel doctrine of suggestion.*[17]

Apart from *Dhvanyaloka,* he has also written many other books. In *Dhvanyaloka* he has referred to two of his previous works, the *Arjunacarita* "The Adventures of Arjuna" and

---

16 Daniel H.H. Ingalls, trans. *The Dhvanyaloka of Anandavardhana with the Locana of Abhinavagupta* (Cambridge, Mass.: Harvard UP, 1990), p. 7.

17 Anandavardhana, Dhvanyaloka (Varanasi: Kashi Sanskrit Series, 1940), pp. 363-364.

Visambanlila, "The Sports of the Bowman Love." His other works include a book on metaphysics called Tattvaloka, one on Buddhist doctrines known as *Dharmottartvivrti* and a poem called "Devisataka."

The purpose of *Visambanlila* was to give instructions in poetry. In describing insentient things as sentient, Anandavardhana remarks, "This is a well-known procedure of great poets and has been described in detail for the instruction of poets in the *Visambanlila*" (4.7). Anandavardhana quotes the verses from *Visambanlila* in *Dhvanyaloka* to illustrate the different varieties of dhvani. So, according to Ingalls, "The *Visambanlila* was Ananda's first work propounding the new doctrine of suggestiveness, in a play or narrative written quite appropriately in Prakrit, for Prakrit was the language in which this style of suggestiveness first became popular and it may well have been from Prakrit that Ananda's interest in dhvani was first stimulated."[18] *Visambanlila* might have been the earliest book illustrating the doctrine of dhvani but *Dhvanyaloka* is the first book which develops this theory systematically.

II

Anandavardhana's dhvani theory was greatly influenced by Bhartṛhari's sphota theory. In *Dhvanyaloka,* Anandavardhana has acknowledged his indebtness to Bhartṛhari's theory. Anandavardhana derived the term "dhvani" which in ancient linguistic term meant sound-unit and applied it to the study of poetry. He, therefore, remarks in *Dhvanyaloka:*

> *...they [the grammarians] gave the name dhvani to the sounds of speech that are heard. In the same manner, men otherwise, who knew the true essence of poetry, have followed the example of the grammarians by giving the title dhvani to that verbal entity which contains a mixture of denotative and denoted elements and which is designated as "a poem." They did so because of the similarity [to acoustical dhvani] in its*

18 Ingalls, 10 - 11.

being a manifestor [of suggested meanings just as the heard sounds manifest words.][19] *[Dhvanyaloka 1.131 A]*

In sphota theory, the sentence is taken as a single semantic unit. Just as a word is divided into roots and suffix, and a phrase is divided into lexical units, a sentence is divided into constituent words to articulate the different grammatical functions. But a sentence as a whole gives the meaning. The sentence meaning is first perceived and then the meanings of the individual words.

The sentence is an indivisible and integral linguistic unit whose meaning is conveyed by an "instantaneous flash of insight or intuition" known as pratibha. Sphota theory speaks in similar terms as the Gestalt theory of psychology in the West. The sentence as a whole exists as the primary/basic unit of meaning, the words do not build up the meaning.

Bhartṛhari considers the logical interpretation of an utterance faulty. So also Anandavardhana tries to look beyond the denotative meaning in a work of art. Sometimes an utterance can give an altogether different meaning from the individual word-meanings put together, according to Bhartṛhari. Anandavardhana's theory of suggestion is an application of Bhartṛhari's linguistic theory in the field of poetics.

Bhartṛhari defines dhvani as "sound-born sounds" which is quite similar to what the Nyaya-Vaisesikas believed. The Nyaya-Vaisesikas described sounds of speech as a series of sounds where only the last sound leads to cognition. Moreover, going by their analogy of the reverberations of a bell, the sounds heard are actually born of other sounds and not the original sound produced by speech organs. This is exactly like ripples created and spread when a stone is thrown in the pond. The last wave that reaches the shore is not directly created by the stone but rather by the preceeding waves, hence it is wave

19 Ingalls 169. (*Dhvanyaloka* 1: 13 A).

produced wave and not a stone-produced wave. Mandana Misra's analogy of a jeweller trying to perceive the genuineness of a precious stone is quite apt here. Like the reverberating bell and the waves produced in the pond, the jeweller's constant gaze at the stone helps in increasing his clarity of perception. Each phase of his gaze adds to newer perception, ultimately the series of perception leading to his cognition. It is the last cognition in the series which leads to his final, complete perception. Bhartṛhari's own analogy of a student trying to learn a verse by-heart is described in the following sloka :

yathanuvakas sloko va sodhatvam upagacchati

avrttya na tu sa granthah pratyavrtti nirspyate.

After repeated readings the student gets the verse by-heart. It is only the last reading which results in his memorizing the verse through a process of storing the number of memory traces of the previous traces.

[Vakyapadiya I.83]

Similarly, the term "dhvani", which Bhartṛhari refers to as "phoneme-manifestor," i.e., which manifests the semantic content of a word through a series of cognition, can be used for denoting the word "suggestion," as it is analogous to the reverberating sounds of the bell.

III

Besides the two well-known functions of language, the literal (abhidha) and the metaphorical (laksana), the Dhvani theorists claimed that there is a third potency of language called suggestion (vyanjana). And suggestion is the proper function of poetic language.

The primary (vacya) meaning of the word is the conventional meaning accepted through usage. The part of the word which conveys the literal meaning is called abhidhavṛtti (denotative function). This is the meaning usually given in the dictionary. The following verse describes the source from which the meaning of a word can be known:

Uaktigraham vyakaranopamanakouaptavakyad vyavaharatauca

vakyasya uesad vivrter vadanti sannidhyatah siddhapadasya vrddhah.

The meaning of the words can be learnt by different ways and the eight ways are: grammar, analogy or comparison, lexicon, rest of the sentence/passage in the context, explanation by the learned, worldly usage, testimony of the trust-worthy and the proximity of a known word.[20]

But the question of an additional meaning raises some semantic problems. The situation when a sentence conveys a meaning not stated by its words arises only when there is a break-down of the sentence's syntactical or logical meaning. So we invoke a secondary meaning. This secondary meaning (bhakta) is an extended meaning which emerges when the primary meaning is inapplicable or impeded.

Abhinavagupta searches for the etymological roots of the word "bhakta" and receives four meanings. The word is derived from "bhakti" which means association. Bhakti is also derived from "bhaga" or "portion." In a sentence like "the boy is a lion" some portion of the lion is attached to the boy like "fierceness" or "might." This transfer of some qualities or gunas to the boy in the above example conveys a metaphor or gauna.

Bhakti is "attachment," "love" or "affect." It is the affective meaning which arises out of the eagerness of the speaker to emphasize a particular aspect of a word sense, like the "might" in the boy. Bhakti also comes from the "blocking" or "breaking" (bhanga) of the primary meaning. The secondary meaning comes to the fore when there is a syntactical incongruity.

20 Jagadisa, *Sabdasaktiprakasika* (Benaras: Kashi Sanskrit Series, 1934), p.103.

Metaphor, as Roman Jakobson defines, is a form of linguistic disturbance in which a word from one linguistic chain or field is transplanted into another in order to heighten the meaning. Poetic language, he believed, is more dislocated and thus more metaphoric in quality.

I. A. Richards, on the other hand, considers all languages to be metaphorical in a broader sense because to speak referentially at all, there is a need to "sort" *this* from *that.* He divides metaphor into two parts: tenor and vehicle. Tenor is the abstract meaning, whereas vehicle is the concrete or figurative one. He illustrates it in the phrase, "Now is the winter of our discontent." Here discontentedness is the tenor and winter is the vehicle. However, the vehicle carries a host of other meanings; it adds the ideas of bitterness and barreness, and so does more than illustrating the tenor.

The Indian philosophers and poeticians have dealt with metaphor in great detail like the Western theorists. The Indian theorists classified indication into two groups—relation-based indication (laksana) and resemblance-based (sadrusyamula) or metaphorical indication (gauni). The relation-based indication (sambandhamula laksana) can be further divided into discarding indication (jahallaksana) and non-discarding indication (ajahallaksana). In discarding indication for example, "the country mourned the death of its leader," "the country" actually means the people of the country. In non-discarding indication the literal sense is not totally abandoned. In the example, "The spears rushed into the city," "spears" actually mean spearmen because the spears also come along with the spearmen.

Mammata sub-divides the metaphorical indication into *saropa* (attributive indication) and *sadhyavasanika* (determinative indication). "The bramhin boy is a fire" is an example of *saropa,* which is a super-imposition of the metaphorical word (fire) on the base (boy). The sentence signifies the similarity of the boy with the fire. As the fire flares up easily so does the boy, who is immediately provoked. Similarly, the phrase, "he is a lion" is an example of saropa. The metaphorical word or object and the base or subject are given an identity each but are mentioned separately. In the determinative variety of indication, the identity of the object merges with the subject. In the example, "he is a real fire," the metaphorical word "swallows" its base. So also in the sentence, "the fox is coming," the cunning of the fox is attributed to the man and the two are merged. The visaya (tenor), i.e., the man and the visayi (vehicle), i.e., the fox are connected with some kind of similarity between them, but instead of being superimposed as in *saropa,* their resemblance is internalized. The metaphors in Western literature have a far greater degree of the "swallowing" effect; for instance, "the fire of Rome addressed the "senate" refers to Cicero. We understand the sentence on the basis of a perceived resemblance.

The rudhilaksana (conventional indication) is similar to the Western term for "dead metaphor." The words, initially used as metaphors, later on became literal. The special semantic effect of laksana (secondary indication) almost ceases in the course of time and it is brought into the sphere of abhidha or common usage.

Sanskrit critics had given a lot of importance to the metaphorical use of language. This is evident in their elaborate exegesis on metaphors (laksana). In Indian poetics, metaphor is considered as a poetic device; a means to an end—the evocation of rasa; whereas, metaphor in the context of Western poetics has deeper significance and applies to the entire range of poetic expression and semantic value.

The type of indication can be represented as:

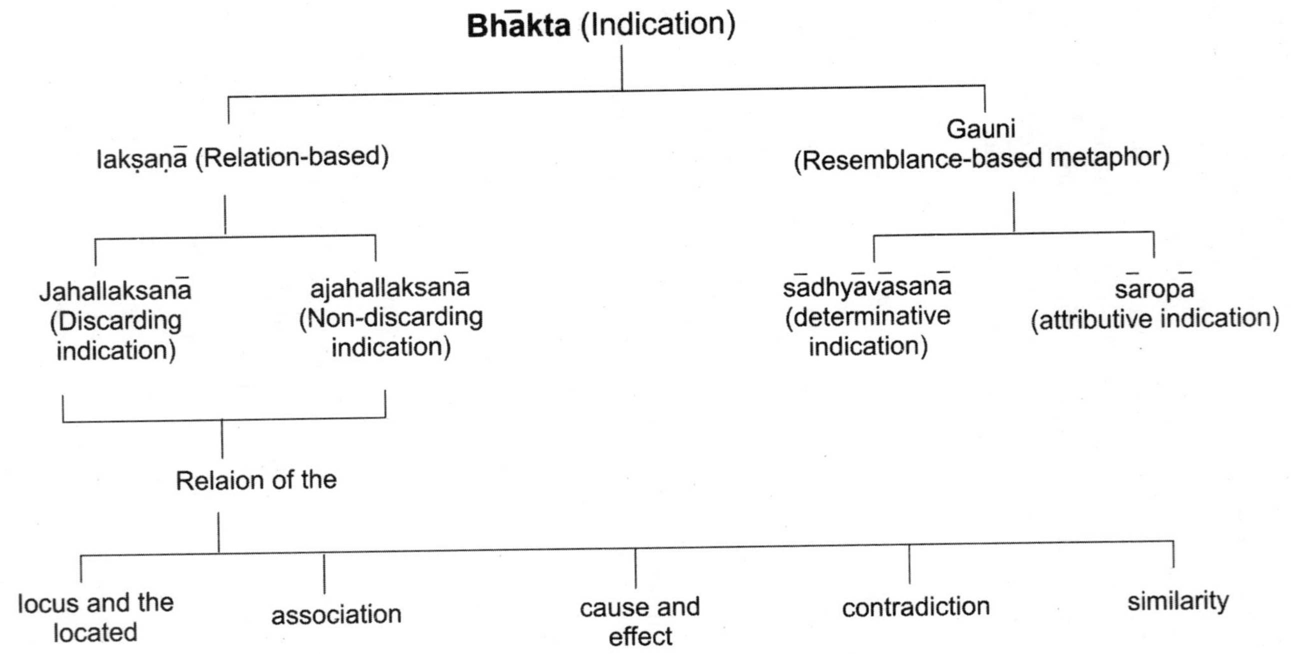
Bhākta (Indication)
lakṣaṇā (Relation-based)
Gauni (Resemblance-based metaphor)
Jahallaksanā (Discarding indication)
ajahallaksanā (Non-discarding indication)
sādhyāvāsanā (determinative indication)
sāropā (attributive indication)
Relaion of the
locus and the located
association
cause and effect
contradiction
similarity

IV

The third function of language, as Anandavardhana says, is dhvani. Dhvani and bhakti are not identical. They have different roles to play in poetry. Vyanjana (suggestion) forms an important part of speech activity, but since Anadavardhana was interested to show vyanjana as an aesthetic element in poetic language, he developed the concept of dhvani which is the predominant vyanjana applied to poetry in its most appealing nature. Dhvani does not occur in the instances where the suggested meaning plays a secondary role.

Anadavardhana does not recognize all unstated meanings as dhvani. Those utterances which are left incomplete either syntactically or in terms of their logical implications are not examples of dhvani, because Anandavardhana does not see any suggestion in logical implication or presupposition.

Dhvani is not any kind of suggestion as found in the figures of speech like samasokti, aksepa, paryayokta, dipaka, sankara, etc. Dhvani is found only where the suggested sense is predominant.

Anandavardhana wanted to bring suggestion into a wholly new semantic category. So he did not accept the older definitions of suggestion which were categorized as figures of speech like samasokti, aksepa, paryayokta, dipaka, sankara. To do this, he invented the distinction between predominant and subordinate suggestion, and he called the predominant suggestion dhvani and left out figure of speech as examples of subordinate suggestion.

He distinguishes three types of poety: true poetry, in which the unspoken part dominates (dhvani kavya); second-grade poetry, in which the unspoken part plays a secondary role (gunibhutavyangya kavya); and third-grade poetry, in which the whole importance is attached to the beauty of language and external figures (citra kavya). True poetry, then, is poetry dominated by suggestion or unexpressed sense. W. M. Urban distinguishes between what poetry says explicitly, and what it says implicitly, "Poetry means what it says, but it does not always say all that it means. There is a great deal of unexpressed reference."[21] The theory of dhvani, like any other new theory, was not without opposition. Anandavardhana had taken many of the objections seriously and refuted them in the first chapter of his book. The major arguments put forward by anti-dhvani theorists, Anandavardhana says, can be classified into three categories. One group denies the existence of any other type of sense except the denotative sense. A word denotes a meaning and there can be no other meaning signified by that word. For them the primary meaning is the one ultimate meaning. They are the abhāvavādins who deny the existence of dhvani. Another group accepts the existence of another sense over and above the primary sense and calls it bhakta, which means an associative or secondary meaning. Bhakta includes both the gauni or the metaphorical and laksana, i.e., the relational sense. Accordingly, the words and their senses can denote the primary meaning (abhidha) and the secondary meaning (laksana). Even if the abhidha or primary meaning does not convey the sense, there is laksana (secondary meaning) which explains everything. So there is no need for inventing another "word" to designate another type of meaning. These bhaktavadins call dhvani a secondary or associated meaning. Still there are others who, while acknowledging the concept of dhvani, say that dhvani is undefinable; it can be exprienced, but cannot by any means be explained. These critics are called anakhyeyavadins.

The abhavavadins disagree with dhvani theorists on three points. They say that poetic language is distinct from scientific /ordinary language and this distinction is brought about by the various tools of embellishment such as figures of speech

---

21 W. M. Urban, *Langauge and Reality* (George Allen and Unwin: London, 1939), p. 489.

(alamkara), qualities (guna), style (riti) and other modes of linguistic ornamentation. The older poeticians had very carefully detailed all the sources that impart beauty to a poem and dhvani does not come under any of these sources that impart beauty. Their second argument is similar to the first: there cannot be any other definition beyond what the early poeticians have reckoned as the source of beauty. The third argument suggests that if dhvani is claimed as a source which provides sweetness and beauty to a poem, it must not be given a separate name and entity. Hence, the argument goes, there is no need to propagate an old theory with the enthusiasm of a new. Of the three groups of critics, the abhavavadins suffer from judgment of error, the bhaktavadins from indecision, and the anakhyeyavadins from insufficient knowledge.

While Anandavardhana's work itself is an answer to the third category of critics, the anakhyeyavadins, he had to make an attempt at refuting the first two—the abhavavadins and the bhaktavadins. His argument against the former was that dhvani is not a mere beauty accessory; rather it is the very soul of poetry. He gives the analogy of a charming woman with beautiful ornaments. The ornaments as external features definitely add to the woman's beauty but charm is something intrinsic to her and does not necessarily depend on the ornaments or individual features. A charming woman can still be charming without the ornaments, but it is not always true for the other way round, i.e., ornament does not bring charm. Similarly, dhvani is the "charm" and alamkaras, guna-riti, etc. are ornaments. The latter may help make a poem attractive but only dhvani brings out its charm.

The bhaktavadins recognized the importance of secondary usage of words but did not believe in the power of suggestion, which was above the secondary usage. Though the logicians tried to explain away all the meanings and functions of words through laksana or the senondary meanings, that was simply not enough to explain the special faculty needed to understand poetry or a piece of literature. Anandavardhana, therefore, distinguishes between the two types of meanings—the explicit and the implicit.

Many later writers, some of whom were also the contemporaries of Abhinavagupta, had strongly opposed the dhvani theory. Mukulabhatta in his *Abhidhavrttimatrka* tried to include dhvani under laksana. He defined laksana as any other sense other than the denotative sense. He broadens his definition of laksana to accommodate all other ideas/ meanings other than the primary meaning. In this sense, dhvani also comes under the purview of laksana and loses its unique identity as a semantic function beyond laksana.

Suggestion, Anandavardhana says, does not occur at the level of metaphoric meaning (bhakta). The metaphoric function is a super-imposed activity of the word located in the "intermediate sense." The literal meaning (abhidha) is directly conventional and is grasped immediately. But the secondary meaning is only indicated due to the intervention of the primary meaning. So some anti-dhvani theorists claim that since secondary meaning, is also an unstated meaning, it can be accepted as a suggestive function. To this, dhvani theorists argue that there is a suggestion which arises out of the secondary meaning. And this suggestion is not subjected to any impediment or cannot be explained by the secondary function. In the example, "the village on the Ganges," there is a syntactical incongruity, because a village cannot exist on the stream of a river. So we admit the secondary meaning here, i.e., "the banks of the Ganges." But "Ganges" also suggest the notion of coolness and sanctity. We do not arrive at the third meaning by resolving the incongruity of the primary meaning. Anandavardhana terms this as the third potency of language called suggestion. Analysing the above example we arrive at the three stages of meaning. First, by the direct relation of the word "Ganges" to its meaning, we understand the stream. The stream takes us to its related meaning, "the banks of the stream," by the indirect relation of one meaning to another meaning. And third, "the banks of the river" suggests a third meaning of "coolness" by further removing the relation of the second meaning to the third.

Mukulabhatta's definition, according to Anandavardhana, is defective because the secondary meaning operates only in the case where the literal sense is impossible, inconsistent and discarded; whereas dhvani can function along with the literal sense. The literal sense can retain its identity where suggestion is intended. Where the secondary meaning conveys only an idea, dhvani conveys either an idea, a figure of speech or an emotion (rasa).

The secondary meaning, according to Anandavardhana, does not occur without abhidha (primary sense). The secondary meaning can function only upon an expressed sense which is not a pre-requisite for vyanjana (suggestion). Suggestion follows intonation, music, dance, gesture and other unarticulated contextual factors.

Dhananjay, the author of *Dasarupaka* (a treatise on drama), and his brother Dhanika, the commentator of the book, have found dhvani equally redundant, as have the Mimamsaskas of the Prabhakara School for very different reasons. The Dhananjay brothers deny dhvani's function claiming that it can be included in "*tatparyavrtti*" (sentential purport). For the followers of the Prabhakara School, on the other hand, all the semantic functions come under the primary function (abhidha), including dhvani.

The concept of *tatparyavrtti* assigns all the functions like secondary meaning and dhvani to the verbal comprehension of a sentence. The individual word meanings lose their identity in a sentence. The cluster of words in a sentence interact with each other and the mutual relation among them, known as samsarga, brings out the meaning. The meaning conveyed by the sentential purport is suggested, according to Dhanika. Abhinavagupta refutes this view by saying that the sentential purport conveys the syntactical connection in a sentence. The syntax conveys the primary meaning. The power of tatparya exhausts after conveying the syntactical connection. Dhvani, therefore, has to be assigned a different function. Dhanika, however, believes that the power of syntax can be extended beyond its logical connection between the different word meanings.

The Prabhakar School, with its doctrine of anvitabhidhana, considers dhvani as the function of abhidha. This transcends the meaning of a word from its mere literal sense. The meaning of a word keeps extending like the course of an arrow which goes further each time it is shot with force and swiftness. The dhvanivadis reject this theory because there would be no restriction on the scope of meanings, and a sentence may never come to a stop. They answer them with the arguments of the abhihitanvayavadins who relate abhidha (denotation) only to its definite conventional meaning. The denotative meaning cannot justify all the meanings in a sentence. If it does so, its objectivity and relevance are lost. There is another level of meaning, which arises not as a logical sequence but due to the power of the context. So for suggestion, another semantic power of the word has to be taken and this is what Anandavardhana call dhvani. He illustrates the scope of suggestion, with the following example:

Go your round freely, gentle monk;
the little dog is gone.
Just today from the thickets by the Goda
Came a fearsome lion and killed him.[22]

[*Dhvanyaloka*, 1.4]

22 Ingalls 83. (*Dhvanyāloka* 1: 4 b.A).

If we go step-by-step from the primary to the secondary to the suggestive meaning, we will find that the primary meaning and the suggested meaning are completely different from each other to the degree of being opposites.

This verse from the point of view of literal meaning is an injunction. A certain lady seems to be the speaker of this verse. A monk comes to the forest everyday to collect flowers for worship. The forest happens to be the secret meeting place of the woman and her lover. She feels disturbed by his intrusion. She wants to prevent him from coming to this place but does not say so directly. Rather she invites him to come to the place more often because the dog who used to frighten him is killed by a lion dwelling in the forest. The monk would be delighted to find the removal of the cause of his fear, but the cause of this removal, i.e., the lion, is more frightening. Obviously the monk wouldn't think of visiting the forest any more. Though the dog is gone something more ferocious has replaced it. The verse suggests a prohibition but is spoken in the form of an invitation. The function of the literal meaning (abhida) ceases after conveying the primary sense, that of invitation: "Go your round freely..." The sense of prohibition has to be conveyed by some other power of words. The secondary usage (laksana) is not applicable here since the primary meaning doesn't get blocked. It is only the power of dhvani which conveys this prohibition. Since dhvani is supposed to be prominent here, the literal meaning is not totally relegated; it gets subordinated to the suggested because the dhvani comes through abhida.

Mammata's comments on the verse seem quite apt. The monk visiting a house for flowers must have been warned by the pet dog. So he goes into the forest. Had he been frightened by the dog in the forest, the woman would not have needed to invent a lion for frightening him further. By asking the monk to go to the house without any hesitation since the dog has been killed, she actually prohibits him from coming to the forest by suggesting that a fierce lion dwells in the forest. The suggestion aims at two things: first, the monk can again go to the house as usual fearlessly; second, by hearing of the lion he will no longer go to the forest. The purpose of the woman and the monk are thus served.

Mahimabhatta's *Vyaktiviveka,* was a fierce and fatal criticism of dhvani theory. A Naiyayika, Mahimabhatta discarded dhvani on the ground that every other function of a word other than the denotative can be included in inference (anumana). Therefore, to invent a new term like dhvani would be superfluous. Rasa is also inferred through the causes and after-effects of emotions. In one of his aphorisms, he alters *Dhvanyaloka's* definition of dhvani to suit his own purpose thus:

Vacyastadanumito vayatrathorthantaram prakauayati

Sambandhatah kutaucit sakavyanumitirityukta.

(Vyaktiviveka, 1:25)

Kavyanumiti or poetic inference occurs wherever the literal meaning reveals a different meaning through inference.[23]

The implied meaning is always inferred from the expressed meaning. So, Mahimabhatta argues, there is no need to create a new function called dhvani. According to him, what the dhvani theorists call suggestion is not a verbal activity at all, but inferential reasoning. When the meaning of a sentence gives rise to another meaning, the other meaning is understood through a further reasoning called inference. He claims that words have only one power: the denotation. The word either surrenders its own meaning or gives rise to another. It only seems to convey different meanings due to differences in the conditions of its use. So Mahimabhatta claims that another meaning of the

23 Mahimabhatta. *Vyaktiviveka,* ed. Madhusudana Misra (Benares: Chowkhamba Sanskrit Series, 1936), p. 105.

word is actually another use of the word. The dhvani theorists contested Mahimabhatta's argument saying that even the inferred meaning is still verbal because the meaning arises from the words. Anandavardhana refutes the anumana (inference) theory on the basis of a lack of an invariable relation between the primary and the suggested sense on which inference depends. For example, the fire in the woods is inferred from the smoke rising there. The relationship/interdependence that exists between the fire and the smoke is absent in the light and the pot. There is no such binding relation between the light and the pot, where the light reveals the pot.

Mahimabhatta's arguments against dhvani theory are based on his postulate that inference is precise, accurate and logical, whereas suggestion is vague and subjective; inference can include suggestion, which can be inferred from the expressed sense. Poetic inference, he says, is based on the expressed sense and rejects other types of extra-linguistic suggestions. What Mahimabhatta ignores is that poetry appeals more to imagination and emotion than to logical reasoning. By excluding the whole range of suggestive language from the scope of poetry, he limits the function of literature and converts it into a logical reasoning. Moreover, only dhvani can explain how negative meaning arises from a positive assertion as the verse "Go round..." in the example above shows. The Mimamsakas view dhvani as part of what they call z, which etymologically means postulation *(apatti)* of fact *(artha)*. It is a means of cognition of a fact which is otherwise incomprehensible. Arthapatti is immediate inference to resolve a logical contradiction. For example, when we use the sentence, "the *fat* Devadutta *never eats* during day time", it can be inferred that he eats at night. Here the contradiction "Fat Devadutta never eats" is resolved by means of arthapatti (immediate inference or material implication) that he must be eating at night. Jesperson has a similar view about the function of suggestion when he says:

> *In all speech activity there are three things to be distinguished: expression, suppression and impression. Expression is what the speaker gives, suppression is what he does not give, though he might have given it and impression is what the hearer receives. It is important to notice that an impression is often produced not only by what is said expressly, but also by what is supressed. Suggestion is impression through suppression.*[24]

After the individual word meanings of a sentence have been conveyed, the samsarga (mutual relation of the words) or the meaning of the sentence is conveyed through the postulation of fact. According to Abhinavagupta, rasa is always suggested. Suggestion is not logical like inference, where the knowledge of one thing is inferred from another.

Now one wonders if the dhvani theorists are not unnecessarily dragging meaning as a mental activity when they try to assign even the motive for metaphor to a special linguistic function. It is difficult to determine where the verbal operation stops and the mental process starts. The dhvani theorists themselves suggest no definite limits to the scope of verbal meaning.

Kuntaka's *Vakroktijivita* and Bhoja's *Srngaraprakasa* cannot be called works on anti-dhvani theory in clear terms. Both try to seek another name for dhvani. Kuntaka's theory of vakrokti or obliqueness of poetic operation is an all-pervasive term which includes figures, style, quality, decorum, suggestion in vakrokti. What dhvani is for Anandavardhana, vakrokti is for Kuntaka. He does not deny the existence of dhvani altogether; rather he alters the definition of the poetic soul (kavyatma) by shifting the emphasis from dhvani to vakrokti.

Bhoja merely uses a different terminology for dhvani and calls it tatparya (purport/intention). He classifies tatparya into

---

24 Otto Jespersen Qtd by W. M. Urban, *Language and Reality* (London: George Allen and Unwin, 1939), p. 12.

three types—abhidhiyamana (denoted sense); pratiyamana (implied sense); and dhvanirupa (a form of suggested sense). He says that the function of tatparya and dhvani are analogous to the field of non-poetic and poetic discourses, respectively.

The dhvani theory accepts the principle of monosemy which requires that a sentence be a complete and unified utterance. A meaningful utterance should have a context. Words, Bhartṛhari says, only have a dictionary meaning, but the meaning of a sentence is its purpose. When context is so integrally related to the meaning of an utterance, Anandavardhana's attempt to limit the purport (tatparya) of a sentence to its grammatical sense and talk of another semantic power, suggestion, to account for what is only the most legitimate meaning of an utterance seems redundant. The meaning and suggestion of a sentence are after all, analysed in terms of contexts.

But unlike the Mimamsakas and Naiyayikas, who believed that meaning depends solely on the words expressed, Anandavardhana established that there are many indicators of meaning, mostly non-verbal, beyond the expressed sense, like intonation, gesture, pure sound, socio-cultural context. In this sense, the expressive symbols (vacakas) and indicative signs (bodhakas) and even music which is emotion devoid of verbal communication, all form part of langauge. Language can include, as Charles Fries remarks, "even the set of deviations from the norms of the sound segments that signal the meaning that a speaker is drunk, the whispering of an utterance that signals the meaning that the content of it is secret, and the unusual distribution that is the cue to a metaphor."[25]

V

In *Dhvanyaloka,* Anandavardhana defines the scope of dhvani as poetic language and classifies its varieties. A major defect

---

25 Charles C. Fries, "Meaning and Linguistic Analysis," *Language* 30 (1954) 67n.

with most of the Sanskrit theorists, including Anandavardhana, was their attempt to present as detailed a classification as possible. One tends to agree with A. B. Keith who said, "In the sub-divisions of which India is so fond there is often much ingenuity in finding legitimate grounds of distinction, but there is always present the tendency to lose sight of the broad and important lines of demarcation while concentrating on minutiae."[26]

Though Anandavardhana does not "lose sight of the broad", his classification of the varieties and sub-varieties of dhvani becomes quite tedious. He claims that the varieties of dhvani are endless but restricts his division of dhvani broadly into two types: avivaksitavacya which is based on laksana (indication) and is also called laksanamula, and vivaksitanyaparavacya, based on abhidha (denotation), is also called abhidhamula. He further sub-divides the two categories of dhvani. This classification of dhvani, according to Anandavardhana, can be represented as:

By delineating the varieties of dhvani that Anandavardhana mentioned in *Dhvanyaloka,* I am particularly interested to show how he demonstrated the distinction between the suggestive and secondary functions of language and how he fought a case for the distinctive use of suggestion in poetic language by providing examples from Indian literary texts.

The two main types of dhvani—avivaksitavacya and vivaksitanyaparavacya—are further sub-divided into two types based on the two varieties of laksana: ajahallaksana corresponding to arthantarasamkramitavacya dhvani where the suggestion is based on progressive denotation, and jahallaksana corresponding to atyantatiraskrtavacya dhvani where the denotation is totally set aside.

26 A. B. Keith, *A History of Sanskrit Literature* (London: Oxford UP, 1920), p. 410.

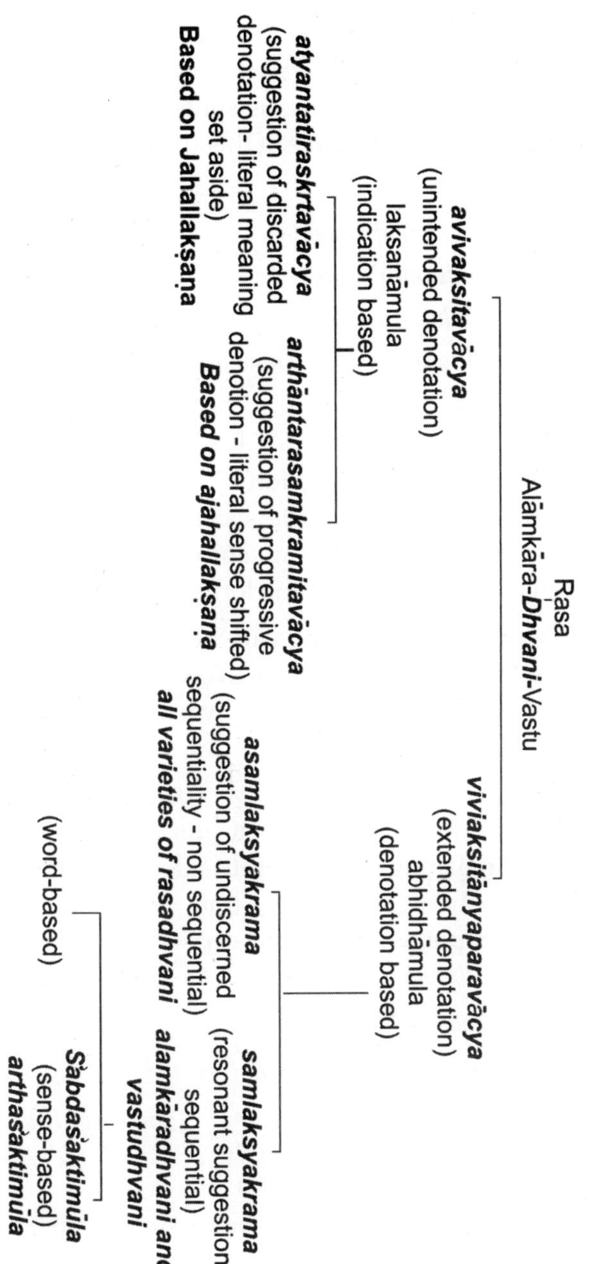
Rasa
Alāmkāra-Dhvani-Vastu
avivaksitavācya
(unintended denotation)
laksanāmula
(indication based)
viviaksitānyaparavācya
(extended denotation)
abhidhāmula
(denotation based)
atyantatiraskrtavācya
(suggestion of discarded
denotation- literal meaning
set aside)
Based on Jahallakṣaṇa
arthāntarasamkramitavācya
(suggestion of progressive
denotion - literal sense shifted)
Based on ajahallakṣaṇa
asamlaksyakrama
(suggestion of undiscerned
sequentiality - non sequential)
all varieties of rasadhvani
samlaksyakrama
(resonant suggestion-
sequential)
alamkāradhvani and
vastudhvani
(word-based)
Śabdaśaktimūla
(sense-based)
arthaśaktimūla

Arthantarasamkramitavacya (suggestion of progressive denotation) is the sub-variety of avivaksitavacya dhvani (unintended denotation) where the literal sense is shifted to something else. Anandavardhana gives an example of this sub-variety :

Virtues blossom
when admired by men of taste.
When graced by the sun's rays
a lotus becomes a lotus.
ravikirananugrhitani kamalani kamalani.[27]

[*Dhvanyaloka*, 2.1b A]

The reiteration of the word "lotus" brings in the meaning forcefully. The literal sense of the second "lotus" is blocked which brings in the secondary meaning and the secondary meaning suggests the beauty of the lotus.

This sub-variety of dhvani can be compared to what Empson calls "the pregnant use of words of the type "A is A"[28] where the logical meaning of a word is weaved into its emotional content.

The second sub-variety of avivaksitavacya is atyantatirasktravacya (suggestion of discarded denotation) where the literal meaning is wholly set aside. Anandavardhana cites examples where sometimes one word suggests the meaning. An example where a word serves as the suggestor is quoted from sage Vyasa :

saptaitah samidhah srihah
these seven are the kindling sticks of royalty.[29]

[*Dhvanyaloka* 3.1 A]

27 Ingalls 105. (*Dhvanyaloka* 2: 16 A).

28 William Empson, The Structure of Complex Words (London: Chatto and Windus, 1951), p. 351.

29 Ingalls 371. (*Dhvanyaloka* 3: 1 A)

To take another example from Valmiki:

ravisamkrantasaubhagyastusarabrtamandalah
nihsvasandha ivadarsacandrama na prakasate.

[Dhvanyaloka 2.1c A]

The sun has stolen our affection for the moon, whose circle now is dull with frost and like a mirror blinded by breath shines no more.[30]

The words "kindling sticks" and "mirror blinded" serve as suggestors in both the examples given above. The kindling sticks (samidhah), used as the base for the sacrificial fire, have completely lost its primary sense and simply mean the seven virtuous deeds which make a king successful. The phrase "mirror blinded" refers to the moon in this case. A mirror is "blinded" only when things are not clearly seen or reflected on it. Ascribing this quality to the moon suggests the loss of beauty, coolness and other properties generally associated with the moon. So the verse suggests that in winter the sun is dearer to us than the moon.

The second variety of dhvani, which is based on abhidha (denotation), is vivaksitanyaparavacya (extended denotation), also known as abhidhamula (denotation based) where the literal meaning is intended but subordinated. This is further sub-divided into asamlaksyakramavyangya (suggestion of non-sequential) and samlaksyakramavyangya (resonant of suggestion). Asamlaksyakrama-vyangya is one where the suggested sense is of undiscerned sequentiality, i.e., the suggested sense is produced without any apparent sequence with the primary sense. In samlaksyakramavyangya, the sequence of the literal and the suggested sense is apparent. The difference between the discernible and undiscernible sequentiality is that in the former, the literal sense is first

30 Ingalls 209. (*Dhvanyaloka* 2: 1 c A).

perceived, and after some time the suggested sense is perceived, whereas in the latter, there is no noticeable gap between the perception of the literal and of suggested sense. Though there is some momentary gap between the two, the perception is so fast that the sequence of the literal and suggested sense becomes imperceptible.

Although Anandavardhana called this second variety, vivaksitanyaparavaya, as the soul of dhvani (*dhvaner atma*), he gives more importance to the sub-variety, asamlaksyakramavyangya (suggestion of undiscarded sequentiality), because the poetic emotions, rasa, etc. are suggested through this. The non-sequentiality of the primary and the suggested sense helps in realizing the rasa immediately in the readers by rousing their sthayibhavas (permanent moods). Rasa can be suggested from a single phoneme, case ending, grammatical number, suffixes, verbal prefixes, tenses, compounds, words, sentences or even the work as a whole.[31] The *Ramayana* and the *Mahabharata* are the two exemplary classical epics, according to Anandavardhana, where the work as a whole suggests a single rasa in spite of the interplay of various emotions suggested by the plurality of suggestors. The *Ramayana* suggests *karuna* rasa and the *Mahabharata santa* rasa.

All varieties of rasadhvani come under asamlaksitakramavyangya (the imperceptible sequence type). The instances of vastu and alamkara dhvani are found in samlaksitakramavyangya (resonant suggestion). Samlaksitakramavyangya, where the suggested sense is perceived after the literal sense, is sub-divided into sabdasaktimula (based on words), arthasaktimula (based on meaning) and sometimes ubhayasaktimula (based on both types). Samlaksitakramavyangya is also compared to the reverberation of a bell. As we hear the resonance of the bell

---

31 Ingalls 453. (*Dhvanyaloka* 3: 16 A).

only after striking the bell, similarly the suggested meaning is apprehended within a momentary interval after the literal meaning is understood. F. Wisemann gives a similar analogy of the chimes of a bell:

> *We seem at times to glimpse behind a word another sense, deeper and half hidden, and to hear faintly the entry of another meaning, in and with which others begin to sound, and all accompany the original meaning of the word like the sympathetic chimes of a bell. Hence, that deep and sonorous ring in words which is lacking in artificial and invented languages; and hence also the multiplicity, the indefiniteness, the strange suggestiveness and evasiveness of so much poetry.*[32]

Anandavardhana quotes from Bana's *Harsacarita* to illustrate the kind of suggestion based on the power of abhidha:

atrantare kusumasamayayugamupasamharannajrmbhat

grismabhidhan: phullamallika dhavalattahaso mahakalah

Meanwhile the long period named summer,

meanwhile the God of Destruction,

When the market stalls are white with the laughter

whose terrible laughter is white

of their blosssoming jasmine flowers,

as jasmine flowers,

expanded as it put an end to the two months of spring.

yawned as he put an end to the aeons of time.[33]

[Harsacarita 19-20]

---

32 F. Wiseman, "Language Strata," in *Logic and Language*, ed. A.G.N. Flew (Oxford: Basil Blackwell, 1951), p. 13.

33 Ingalls 302. (*Dhvanyaloka* 2: 21e A).

I have used two types of fonts to represent the denotative sense and the suggested sense. Bana is actually describing the transition of seasons from spring to summer. Whereas this seems to me an example of an implicit metaphor, Anandavardhana considers the verse as having a suggested meaning. He thinks that since there is no word like "as" relating the two meanings in the form of a figure of speech like simile or metaphor, we should look at the suggested meaning.

Arthasaktimuladhvani is a type of suggestion based on the power of meaning. Whereas sabdasaktimula dhvani suggests either an idea or a figure of speech. Arthasaktimuladhvani is usually appreciated for its suggestion of emotions, rasa, etc. Anandavardhana gives a beautiful example of arthasaktimuladhvani:

evamvadini devarsau parsve pituradhomukhi

lilakamalapatrani ganayamasa parvati

[Kalidasa, Kumara Sambhava, 6.84]

While the heavenly visitor was speaking, Parvati,

standing with lowered face beside her father,

counted the petals of the lotus in her hand.[34]

While the sage and Parvati's father are discussing Parvati's marriage with Siva, Parvati is delighted at hearing this. But she cannot express her delight in front of the elders because it was considered indecent. Her gestures, however, of lowering her face and counting the lotus petals definitely suggest her bashful concealment of emotions (sthayibhava) of love like joy, fear, anxiety, eagerness. The verse does not directly suggest sr̥ngara rasa but by suggesting the emotions (vyabhicaribhavas) associated with srngara rasa like agitation (avega), instability (capalya), shyness, the verse, in a way, suggests sr̥ngara rasa.

---

34 Ingalls 311. (*Dhvanyaloka* 2: 22 A).

All Indian theorists invariably agree that the ultimate aim of reading poetry is the relishing of rasa. Bhatta Lollata, Anandavardhana, Abhinavagupta, Mammata, Bhoja and Visvanatha borrowed Bharata's rasa theory and applied it to poetry. However, it was Anandavardhana who said that rasa was the end for the attainment of which dhvani should be the means. A poem of extraordinary charm must, therefore, have a suggested rasa. Since emotions are psychological states, they cannot be anyway directly conveyed. Emotions are always suggested. So creating a separate semantic activity to suggest emotions is not required.

VI

Anandavardhana discusses three types of dhvani: Vastu-dhvani, alamkara-dhvani and rasa-dhvani. Vastu-dhvani is the suggestion of a thing or an idea; alamkara-dhvani is the one where a figure of speech or alamkara is suggested; rasa dhvani is where a rasa is suggested. Of these he claims for rasa dhvani a superior status.

Abhinavagupta, however, differentiates between two types of dhvani: a workaday variety; the other used specifically in poetry. He claims that all the other types of dhvani, except rasa dhvani, come under the first category. He further divides the first category into vastu-dhvani and alamkāra-dhvani. They can be expressed verbally through a literal form. But this cannot hold true for rasa-dhvani. Abhinavagupta remarks:

> *...rasa is something that one cannot dream of expressing by the literal sense. It does not fall within workaday expression. It is, rather, of a form that must be tasted by an act of blissful relishing on the part of a delicate mind through the stimulation (anuraga) of previously deposited memory elements which are in keeping with the vibhavas and anubhavas, beautiful because of their appeal to the heart, which are transmitted by [suggestive] words [of the poet]. The suggesting of such a sense is called rasadhvani and is*

> *found to operate only in poetry. This, in the strict sense of the word, is the soul of poetry.*[35]

However, the theory of rasa-dhvani has also parallels in Aristotle's theory of "mimesis-catharsis" and Longinus' "sublime-transport." The complementary terms, dhvani/ mimesis/sublime and rasa/catharsis/transport are required for the realization of art-experience. Here the first bunch of terms suggests what inheres "objectively" in the work and the latter category describes the impact on the readers. Longinus's concept of the "sublime" comes quite close to "dhvani" theory. Longinus defines the sublime as "elevated language" or that which "consists of a certain excellence and distinction in expression" and implies that it is from this source that the greatest writers acquire their pre-eminence." He further explains this process:

> *For the effect of elevated language is not to persuade the hearers, but to entrance them; and at all times, and in every way, what transports us with wonder is more telling than what merely persuades or gratifies us.*[36]

Longinus can be said to be the classical antecedent of the New Critics. The process of anuramana, described by the dhvani theorists is like the sound-waves produced in the ringing of the bell. For this effect of resonance, the referential language has to be different from the emotive language because the "rigour-haunted" and "economy-ridden" language, according to I. A. Richards, cannot account for the emotive language.

Aristotle's mimesis and Longinus's term for imitation are two quite different notions. Mimesis is the imitation of nature or human nature, while for Longinus imitation is the stimulus derived by younger writers from the older masters. Longinus's notion sounds similar to what the Indian theorists believed

35 Ingalls 81. (*Locana* 1: 4a A).

36 Longinus, *On the Sublime*, ed. T.S. Dorsch (London: Penguin Books, 1969), p. 33.

that "*pratyaksa* is not the *pramana*," that is, creativity should not be a mere imitation of the living/present entities but should be handed down by the canons and past practice of older masters. Longinus's idea and the Indian concept of imitation anticipate the neo-classical doctrine, "to study classics is to study nature."[37] It also finds parallel in T. S. Eliot's concept of "Tradition" where the past is the reckoning force for the present.

Eliot also talks something similar to the Sanskrit critics regarding the functions of poetry:

> *I suppose it will be agreed that every good poet has something to give us besides pleasure, there is always the communication of some new experience, or some fresh understanding of the familiar, or the expression of something we have experienced but have no words for, which enlarges our consciousness or refines our sensibility.... Without producing these two effects it simply is not poetry.*[38]

The aim of poetry, besides giving aesthetic pleasure, is also to instruct ethical values (purusartha). While the Vedas (sastras) and history also instruct, they do so as a teacher and a friend, respectively. But the instructions kavya (literature) gives are like those of a loving wife (kantasammitataya upadesa) who is irresistably sweet. Abhinavagupta admits that aesthetic enjoyment is the main goal of poetry but the instructions given by poetry are different from instructions given by other types of literature, i.e., poetry has a moral value; it is spritually instructive. Abhinavagupta sounds much like the New Critics, like I. A. Richards, for whom poetry has a therapeutic value and takes the position of religion and morality in the modern age.

37 Longinus 35.

38 T. S. Eliot, *Poetry and Poets* (London: Faber, 1957), p. 18.

The *rasa* theory was an attempt to indicate the character of the emotional effect, i.e. the nature of enjoyment experienced by the spectator in witnessing a play. Hence, in ultimate analysis, it was an attempt to define the purpose of drama, or in later aesthetic thought, of any work of art, for in Indian aesthetics, artistic delight in all cases is comprehended in terms of rasa. Aesthetic experience is, therefore, "the act of tasting of the rasa, of immersing oneself in it to the exclusion of all else."[39]

Bharata has stated in the sixth chapter of *Natyasastra* the process of realization of rasa. Rasa is born out of the combination of *vibhavas* (causes of emotions), *anubhavas* (after effects of emotions) and *vyabhicaribhava* (transient moods) with *sthayibhava* (basic emotions). *Vibhavas* are of two kinds, *alambana* and *uddipana.*

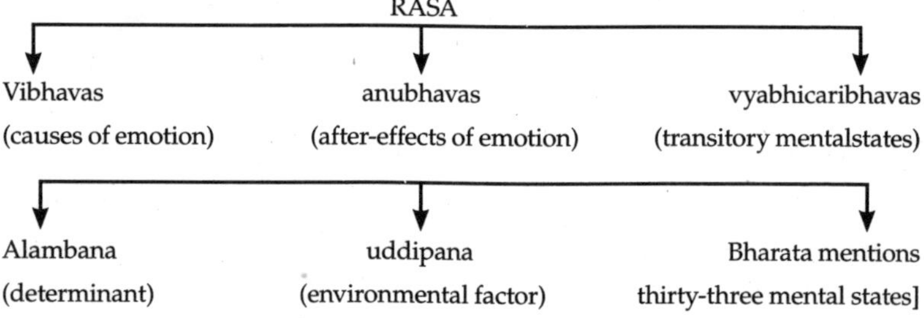

Alambana is the determinant towards which an emotion is manifested, such as the hero and the heroine. *Uddipana* are environment factors that excite an emotion, for example, spring, flowers, moonlight, etc. *Anubhavas* are the external manifestations of emotion such as the movement of the eyebrows, glances and smile. The *vyabhicaribhavas* are the accessory moods which come and go helping in the manifestation of rasa; they are transitory mental states that accompany and help intensify the dominant and permanent emotional mood—the *sthayibhava.*

---

39 Raniero Gnoli, *The Aesthetic Experience According to Abhinavagupta* (Varanasi: Chowkhamba Sanskrit Series, 1968) XIX.

Bharata mentions thirty-three transient moods and eight permanent emotional moods: the eight basic emotions corresponding to the eight rasas are:

Sthayins	***Rasas***
Rati (the sexual emotion)	*Srngara* (love)
Hasa (laughter/amusement)	*Hasya* (the comic)
Soka (grief/distress)	*Karuna* (pathos)
Krodha (anger)	*Raudra* (anger)
Utsaha (masterfuleness/energy)	*Vira* (the heroic)
Bhaya (fear)	*Bhayanaka* (fear)
Jugupsā (disgust)	*Bibhatsa* (disgust)
Vismaya (wonder)	*Adbhuta* (wonder)
Sama (subsidence)	*Santa* (serenity)

The basic emotion, when not properly and adequately nourished, does not turn into rasa; it remains in the state of emotion. In the same way, any feeling other than the basic emotions always remains an emotion and does not reach the stage of rasa. It is also said that when a basic emotion like love has as its alambana-vibhava (determinant), a king or a god, and not lovers, it evokes no rasa but remains only a feeling.

When *rasa* or *bhava* (emotion) is evoked inappropriately, *rasabhasa* or *bhavabhasa* (a semblence of rasa or emotion) is the result. For example, if love in the hero is not reciprocated, or if the emotion is depicted in another person other than the hero, the result is sr̥ngarabhasa (the semblence of the emotion of love) and not the full-fledged sr̥ngara rasa. A manifestation of *bhava* under similar conditions would result in *bhavabhasa*.

It is the basic emotion that becomes rasa, but in the process it undergoes a transformation and takes a totally different form. Rasa is quite different from emotion. Rasa is in all instances pleasurable, while emotions are painful in some instances. If rasa were painful, nobody would be inclined to experience it. Rasa is an experience whose nature is alaukika, i.e., transcending the bounds of worldly experience. As Abhinavagupta explains:

Rasa is not of the nature of an ordinary effect, for it ceases to exist when vibhavas are withdrawn, nor is it a preformed product which is merely revealed by vibhavas and others. Rasa does not exist before the representation of vibhavas. Rasa is a unitary entity in which any traces of vibhavas and others are not perceived individually. In a drink prepared of sugar, pepper and other ingredients, there exists a unique sweetness, and the tastes of the individual ingredients are not discernible. So is rasa.[40]

The following passage from Eliot has resonances with the Indian theory of *rasa*:

The effect of a work of art upon the person who enjoys it is an experience different in kind from any experience not of art. It may be formed out of one emotion, or may be a combination of several; and various feelings, inhering for the writer in particular words or phrases or images, may be added to compose the final result. Or, great poetry may be made without the direct use of any emotion whatever, composed out of feelings solely.[41]

Though the Indian theorists would talk of one dominant rasa throughout a work of art, they would agree with Eliot about poetic genres suggesting "various feelings," i.e., transient moods like devotional (bhakti) poems or poems on renunciation (nirveda) without using one dominant emotion.

Bharata's theory defining the process of rasa realization is interpreted differently by scholars. The four interpretations which have gained the widest acceptance are: *utpattivada* (cause and effect relationship); *anumitivada* (process of logical inference); *bhuktivada* (process of universalization) and *abhivyaktivada*; put forward by Bhatta Lollata, Sri Sankuka, Bhatta Nayaka and Abhinavagupta, respectively.

---

40 Gnoli 274.

41 T. S. Eliot, *Points of View*, ed. John Hayward (London: Faber, 1941), p. 30.

Lollata considered the manifestation of rasa as a result of an intensification of the basic emotions. Thus, the emotion and rasa stand in the relation of cause and effect; when an emotion is intensified to the highest pitch, it turns into rasa. The *rasa* primarily resides in the character and secondarily in the actor who imagines himself the character. It does not reside in the poet or in the spectator.

The theory of logical inference of Sri Sankuka was based on the premise that rasa is a process of logical inference, where the spectator infers rasa when the vibhavas or causes of emotions are placed before him. The actor by his acting imitates the character of the hero, and the spectator identifies the actor with the hero, which leads him to the inference of rasa. A. Sankaran remarks on this point: "The emotions of the hero in ordinary life are manifested by causes, bodily effects and accompanying mental states and these when imitated by the actor become *vibhavas* etc. The emotion that the audience have is but a reflex (anukara) of, the real emotional mood–sthayibhava–of the character; and is called by a different name, viz. rasa."[42]

The theory of Bhatta Nayaka was an improvement on the theories of both Lollata and Sri Sanuka and paved the way for the more competent theory of Abhinavagupta. In Bhatta Nayaka's opinion, rasa is neither produced nor manifested. If emotion is evoked as it is, none would experience pleasure from such rasas as *Karuna* (pathos) or *bhayanaka* (fear). The experience would certainly be distasteful. He postulated three functions of words– (i) *abhidha* (denotation); (ii) *bhavakatva* (power of generalization); (iii) *bhojakatva* (process of relishing the generalized emotion). *Abhidha* is the power of denotation. *Bhavakatva* is typical of poetic language, it is the power of generalization through which the emotions are grasped in a universal way, without any specific individual properties, leading to a generalization called *sadharanikarana* (universal transpersonalization.) Through the

42 A. Sankaran, The Theories of Rasa and Dhvani (Madras: University of Madras, 1929), p. 100.

third function, bhojakatva (generalization), the emotion thus generalized is enjoyed, and this experience is always pleasurable.

Abhinavagupta tried to refute Bhatta Nayaka's theory because it was in conflict with the dhvani theory. Nevertheless, he benefits greatly from it, for his own interpretations of the *rasa* theory incorporates the salient features of Bhatta Nayaka's interpretation.

Abhinavagupta differs from Bhatta Nayaka on the point that word possesses two functions called *bhavakatva* and *bhojakatva* (the process of generalization and relishing). He rejects these functions on the basis that there is no valid authority for accepting them as different functions. His contention is that *bhavakatva* is not different from vyanjana (suggestion). The process of generalization is accomplished through the suggestive function in poetry, and hence there is no need to postulate another notion. Regarding the other function of relishing the emotion, Abhinavagupta contends that this is none other than the enjoyment of rasa or *rasapratiti*. The responsive reader has within him/her latent impressions of emotions experienced previously. These are known as purvavasana. The sthayibhavas lie dormant in the form of vasana. When he reads or witnesses a clear representation of appropriate causes, after-effects and accompanying mental states of emotions, these latent impressions are evoked and developed to such a pitch that they are realized in their universal form, devoid of personal or individual qualities (sadharanikarana). In this impersonalized state, the feelings are always pleasurable, and are enjoyed in the form of rasa.

Abhinavagupta speaks of seven obstacles lying in the way of rasa-realization. They are all the extraneous elements which break the unity of a state of consciousness, the unity that is required for the sahrdaya (connoisseurs) to acquire the correct mood to enjoy rasa.

The first of these obstacles has been described as the lack of adequate realization of probability of things. The incidents presented in a literary composition must convince for their probability.

The second and third obstacles against enjoying a rasa laid down by Abhinavagupta pertain to the circumstances where the reader is unable to experience a generalized state of emotions. If the reader realizes the emotions existing in himself or in some other specific individuals, no generalization is possible. Again, if the reader is preoccupied with his own sorrows or joys, then too he is unable to react to the emotions presented in literature and to generalize them.

The fourth and fifth obstacles pertain to the lack of clarity of perception of things presented before the reader. If the causes and after-effects of emotions are not realized immediately, or if they are not sufficiently clear, the evocation of rasa is hindered. The absence of a properly brought out dominant element is the sixth obstacle to rasa. If the factors like causes, after-effect of emotions and the accompanying mental states are presented individually, a doubt may possibly arise as to which emotion is intended to be developed. This doubt is the seventh and last obstacle of rasa realization.

J. N. Mohanty gives a graphic representation of all the four interpretations of Bharata's *Natyasastra* presenting the process of rasa realization and trans-personalization (sadharanikarana).[43]

According to Mohanty, Lollata had a simplified view on rasa. For Lollata, rasa is the emotion intensified and developed to the highest degree and it is located in the dramatic character. Lollata held that rasa is physically produced (utpatti), whereas the other critics, Sankuka, Bhatta Nayaka and Abhihavagupta, believed that rasa was either manifested or relished. The audience relish the aesthetic bliss suggested in the play.

---

43 J. N. Mohanty, *Classical Indian Philosophy* (Oxford: Oxford UP, 2000), pp. 136–137.

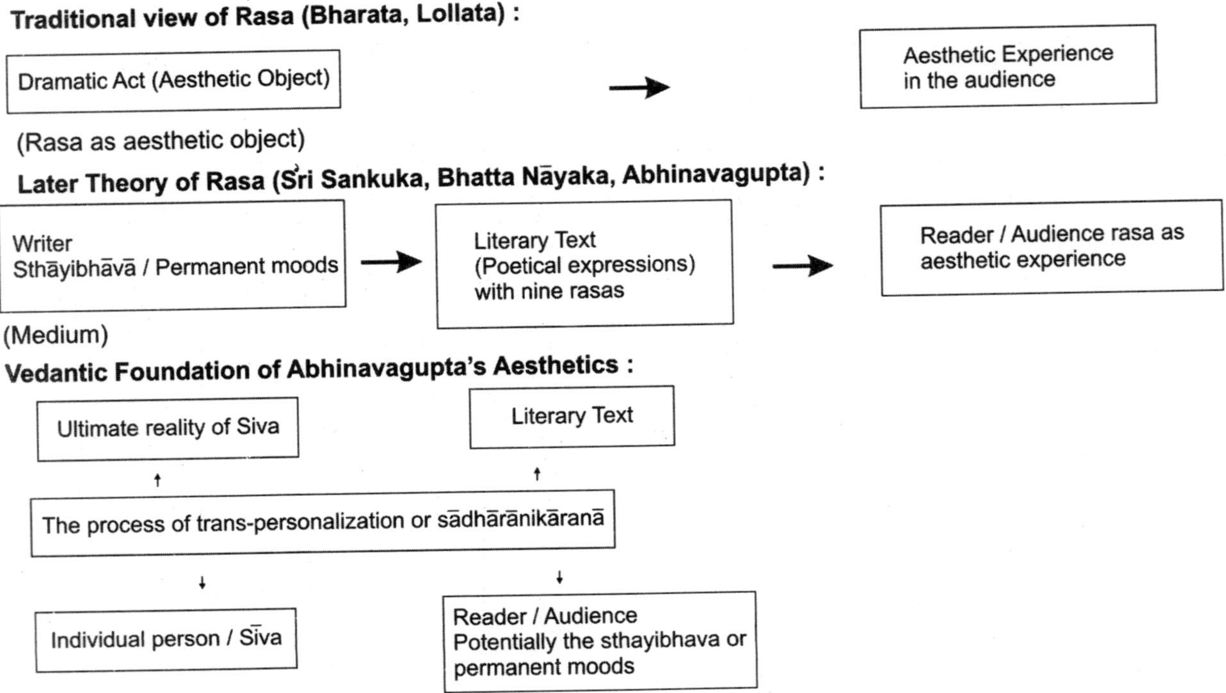
Traditional view of Rasa (Bharata, Lollata) :
Dramatic Act (Aesthetic Object)
Aesthetic Experience in the audience
(Rasa as aesthetic object)
Later Theory of Rasa (Śri Sankuka, Bhatta Nāyaka, Abhinavagupta) :
Writer Sthāyibhāvā / Permanent moods
Literary Text (Poetical expressions) with nine rasas
Reader / Audience rasa as aesthetic experience
(Medium)
Vedantic Foundation of Abhinavagupta's Aesthetics :
Ultimate reality of Siva
Literary Text
The process of trans-personalization or sādhārānikāranā
Individual person / Sīva
Reader / Audience Potentially the sthayibhava or permanent moods

Mohanty analyses the impact of the Advaita philosophy of the Saivite school on Abhinavagupta's interpretation of rasa. According to Abhinavagupta, rasa is essentially pleasurable, it is a state of bliss, self realization or self fulfillment. The state of bliss is equivalent to spiritual illumination where the spectator is raised above the sensual elements with refined sensiblilities. Abhinavagupta compares the relation between the aesthetic efficacy of the text and the reader's aesthetic experience with the relation between the *Upanisads* and knowledge of Brahman. According to the Saivite school of philosophy, to which Abhinavagupta belonged, every form of pleasure is a manifestation of the spirit. But Abhinavagupta puts spirital bliss at a higher position than rasa and this, I think, is because aesthetic bliss unlike the spiritual bliss is not a permanent state of joy. Nevertheless, aesthetic experience is different from the spiritual experience only in quality and not in essence.

Visvanath says that rasa, experienced by sensible men, is indivisible, self-manifested, compounded of joy consciousness, and is closely related to the realization of the brahman. This lofty and sophisticated concept of the response to art has the Western equivalent in the aesthetic experience: "It is emotion objectified, universalized; and raised to a state where it becomes the object of lucid disinterested contemplation and is transfigured into serene joy."[44]

I. A. Richards describes this aesthetic experience as "a systematization of impulses," which is a pre-condition of happiness. He does not call it "pleasure" but admits that it is a state of gratification. Richards uses behavioural psychology to explicate his theory. He defines aesthetic experience as something which satisfies the largest number of impulses. An ideal mental state, for him, is one where the largest number of appentencies are fulfilled, and the mind attains a state of

44 Krishna Rayan, "Rasa and Objective Correlative," in *Critical Thought*, ed. S.K. Desai and G.N. Devy (New Delhi: Sterling Publishers, 1987), p.114.

calmness. He talks of a term "synaesthesia" which is the effect of poetry on the immediate consciousness where the opposites are reconciled. The reader attains harmony with the mundane world. "Synaesthesia" cannot be compared with rasa. Rasa is a transcendental joy. Aesthetic bliss is an impersonal or universalized experience, a state of the psyche but does not transcend the psyche. I would agree with the Indian poeticians who believed that aesthetic experience is a pleasant experience of an imaginative recreation of an emotion.

All the Indian schools of poetics borrowed Bharata's rasa theory, developed it and applied it to poetry. The Sanskrit critics invariably agreed that the ultimate aim of reading poetry is the relishing of the rasa. But where Anandavardhana significantly differed from the traditional Alamkara school was when he says that rasa is always suggested. The relation between vibhavas (object) and rasa is that of the suggestor (vyangya) and the suggested (vyanjaka), whereas the followers of the Alamkara school included rasa as an ornament of poetic language. But Anandarvardhana's theory that rasa is always suggested has a wider efficacy because stating a rasa directly by its name like sr̥ngara or karuna fails to produce the feeling or apprehension of the emotions like love or pathos. Rasa is always relished when it is suggested or conveyed through objects.

Vibhava or object is the most important element in determining the rasa or aesthetic experience. Most of the theoretical systems in India and the West accept vibhavas or objectification as a valid method of presenting objects in the phenomenal world for idealized, de-individualized, purely affectively efficient equivalents of them. These vibhavas (objects) are the objective and stated material in the literary work; the emotion is the subjective and suggested product arrived at within the reader.

For T. S. Eliot, emotion can be expressed in art only through "objective correlative." Emotion, the content of property, strikes the readers through the organized and patterned form of the poem. The adequate and integral expression of the poet's emotion is termed "objective correlative." In his essay on Hamlet he remarks:

> *Mr. Robertson is undoubtedly correct in concluding that the essential emotion of the play is the feeling of a son towards a guilty mother... The only way of expressing emotion in the form of art is by finding an 'objective correlative'; in other words, a set of objects, a situation, a chain of events which shall be the formula of that particular emotion; such that when the external facts, which must terminate in sensory experience, are given, the emotion is immediately evoked... The artistic 'inevitability' lies in this complete adequacy of the external to the emotion; and this is precisely what is deficient in Hamlet. Hamlet (the man) is dominated by an emotion which is inexpressible, because it is in excess of the facts as they appear... His disgust is occasioned by his mother, but... his mother is not an adequate equivalent for it... And it must be noticed that the very nature of the donnees of the problem precludes objective equivalence. To have heightened the criminality of Gertrude would have been to provide the formula for a totally different emotion in Hamlet; it is just because her character is so negative and insignificant that she arouses in Hamlet the feeling which she is incapable of representing.*[45]

And this is exactly what the dhvani theorists would say regarding the suggestibility of rasa or emotion. According to Anandavardhana, the essential emotion here signifies the dominant rasa. The objective correlative of a rasa, that is, a set of objects, a situation, a chain of events, involves the combination of causes and after-effects of emotions and the transient mood.

---

45 T. S. Eliot, *Selected Essays* (London: Faber, 1932), p. 145.

Hamlet's disgust is one of the eight basic emotions, and Gertude is the alambana-vibhava or determinant of Hamlet's disgust. The inadequacy of the external objects to the emotion is, according to Mammata, rasa-dosa, while Ksemendra would term it as anaucitya (inappropriate). Eliot's passage on Hamlet can be translated into the rhetorics of Sanskrit criticism, especially in terms of Anandavardhana's theory of rasa-dhvani. But there is one major difference between the two: while Anandavardhana would have disqualified the play as a failure on the dramatist's part, Eliot says that the "failure" inheres in the situation in the play. Apart from this difference, the central proposition of Eliot that emotions are suggested through their sensuous equivalents is similiar to the Sanskrit theory of rasa-dhvani.

I. A. Richards and Susanne Langer do not think that the referential object suggests emotion. Langer, however, has a slightly different view of objectification when she says that the object is the work of art itself:

> *How can we capture, hold and handle feelings so that their content may be made conceivable and presented to our consciousness in universal form without being understood in the strict sense, i.e., by means of concepts? The answer is: We can do it by creating objects wherein the feelings we seek to hold are so definitely embodied that any subject confronted with these objects, and emphatically disposed toward them cannot but exprience a non-sensuous appreciation of the feelings in question. Such objects are called works of art.*[46]

However, to me, Eliseo Vivas' objection to Eliot's concept that a set of objects can possibly express or evoke the same "particular emotion" seems viable. Eliot demands a particularity of relationship between the object and emotion. Unlike Eliot, Abhinavagupta shows that the relationship

46 Susanne Langer, *Feeling and Form* (London: Routledge and Kegan Paul, 1952), p. 21.

between the object and emotion is always suggestive. It is a relatively complex and loose process of signification.

In socio-cultural context, the object-emotion bond is flexible, but Wimsatt and Beardsley state how poetry gives this bond stability and continuity:

> *Poetry is a way of fixing emotions or making them more permanently perceptible when objects have undergone a functional change from culture to culture, or when as simple facts of history they have lost emotive value with the loss of immediacy. Though the reasons for emotion in poetry may not be so simple as Ruskin's "noble grounds for the noble emotions," yet a great deal of constancy for poetic objects of emotion—if we will look for constancy—may be traced through the drift of human history.*[47]

For example, Shakespeare's Shylock is an object of pathos or karuna rasa and the murder of the king in *Macbeth* is an object of horror or bhayanaka.

Cleanth Brooks notes how objective correlatives differentiate themselves into two types representing two basic ways of presenting emotion.[48] The first type consists in discursively presenting a sequence of events which provides the reason for the emotion; the second type consists in providing a symbol which is the suggestive equivalent of the emotion. He says that the two types are not mutually exclusive. Brooks believes that there is an evolution from the first type to the second, and this transforms a literary work from the "factual" to the "purely qualitative."

Though the dhvani theorists talked about events, motives, external causes as objects for suggesting rasa, they were not

---

47 W.K. Wimsatt, *The Verbal Icon* (New York: University of Kentucky Press, 1954), p.37.

48 W.K. Wimsatt and Cleanth Brooks, *Literary Criticism: A Short History* (London: Routledge, 1957), pp. 672, 676.

aware of the notion of a symbol which, I think, could have enriched their theory of suggestion. The New Critics seem more privileged than the dhvani theorists because of integrating symbol into Eliot's formulation of objective correlative.

W. K. Wimsatt and Monroe C. Beardsley also emphasise that in poetry emotions are presented in objects:

> *The emotions correlative to the objects of poetry become a part of the matter dealt with—not communicated to the reader like an infection or disease, not inflicted mechanically like a bullet or knife wound, not administered like a poison, not simply expressed as by expletives or grimaces or rhythms, but presented in their objects and contemplated as a pattern of knowledge.*[49]

Wimsatt and Beardsley make a distinction between what we call in Sanskrit poetics *laukika-karanas* and *vibhavas*. *Laukika-karanas* are objects in real life and are factual reasons for intense emotion. But *vibhavas* are objects in fictitious or poetic statement and suggest an emotion that is specific, permanent and less intense but "far wider." This emotion is suggested by "association" like metaphor.

Abhinavagupta as well as Wimsatt and Beardsley consider objects of emotion as the the main concern of critical discourse. Objects (vibhavas), for them, is an inclusive term which includes plot, character, style, theme and language. Abhinavagupta believes that all the objective contents of poetry should aim at *rasaucitya* which is aesthetic and amoral. Abhinavagupta had perhaps anticipated what Wimsatt and Beardsley said at a later time:

> *The more specific the account of the emotion induced by a poem, the more nearly it will be an account of the reasons for emotion, the poem itself, and the more reliable it will be as an account of what the poem is likely to induce in other-*

49 W.K. Wimsatt, *The Verbal Icon*, p.37.

> *sufficiently informed-readers. It will in fact supply the kind of information which will enable reader to respond to the poem. It will talk not of tears, prickles, or other physiological symptoms, of feeling angry, joyful, hot, cold, or intense, or of vaguer states of emotional distubrance, but of shades of distinction and relation between objects of emotion.*[50]

Taking into account of both what Abhinavagupta said and the New Critics reiterated later, I think, literary studies should concern itself with the internal objective structures in the work that evoke emotion.

Eliot criticises the Romantic tradition of expressing the poet's personal emotion and believes that poetry is not the expression of personality but an escape from personality. This escape from personality is nothing but the impersonalization of the emotions into rasa. The poet's "personal emotions" are universalized and become universal emotions. The example of Valmiki's utterance of the first verse is a compelling evidence of such an escape from personality. Valmiki is overcome with grief at the killing and separation of the curlew's mate and utters these words:

May you never find honour, Nisada,

for everlasting years,

who have shot the loving mate

from this pair of curlew birds.

(Ramayana 1.2.14)

The hunter shots one of the pair of the mating birds and is thus cursed by Valmiki. Tha *soka* (grief) of Valmiki turns into *sloka* that is the first verse. It is believed that the word "*soka*" is etymologically responsible for the word "*sloka*."

---

50 W.K. Wimsatt, *The Verbal Icon*, p.34.

Soka (grief) is a painful experience and one never enjoys or relishes this emotion, but rasa is bliss or ananda. *Soka* turns into *Sloka* and gives delight (ananda). Now what is it that transforms *Soka* into *ananda*? Anandavardhana says, it is the rasa which is blissful. Grief which is the basic emotion or bhava of karunarasa (compassion) is intensified and heightened and thus turns into rasa. The poet first felt the grief of the bird, then relished its grief by a process of turning his own grief into an impersonalized and universal grief. Abhinavagupta comments: "By relishing the bird's sorrow he has lost his own griefs within them."[51]

Anandavardhana and Abhinavagupta differ on the issue whether the rasa already existed in the poet while uttering this verse. Their argument focus on various aspects of rasa-realization and the process of transformation of bhava into rasa. Abhinavagupta tend to disagree with Anandavardhana who says that Valmiki composed the verse in grief. Abhinavagupta argues that any composition is impossible while a person is suffering pain or grief. The poet did suffer agony but his agony was transformed into compassion which was responsible for the composition. The transformation, however, was quite fast.

For Anandavardhana *Soka* is intensified and becomes karunarasa. Abhinavagupta says that rasa is realized when basic emotion or *bhava* of the person becomes one with whom s/he is empathizing. It is a melting process; melting of one's basic emotion. The slain curlew's mate's grief found response in the poet's grief. This correspondence of the poet's grief with that of the bird thus becomes impersonalized and universalized and turns into rasa. Since rasa is the aesthetic enjoyment of an emotion, *soka* when aesthetically relished, transforms itself into karunarasa. Abhinavagupta, therefore, remarks:

> *Where we have the basic emotion grief, a thought-trend that fits with the vibhavas and anubhavas of this grief, if it is*

51 Ingalls 110. (Locana 1: 4 g).

relished (literally, if it is chewed over and over), becomes a rasa and so from its aptitude (towards this end) one speaks of (any) basic emotion as becoming a rasa. For the basic emotion is put to use in the process of relishing: through a succession of memory elements it adds together a thought-trend which one has already experienced in one's own life to one which one infers in another's life, and so establishes a correspondence in one's heart.[52]

Daniel H. H. Ingalls adds that "the sympathetic response (*hrdayasamvada*) to the vibhavas and anubhavas is said to 'transcend the experience of the workaday world' (2.4L). Where the Westerner may think of empathy as rendering Hamlet's grief and problems as his own, Abhinava thinks of the process of empathy with, say Rama, or with the grieving bird, as liberating one's personal memory of grief into a universal, impersonal flavor."[53]

Poetry transforms the basic emotions, which otherwise cause pain or pleasure to human beings in their everyday life, to something aesthetically pleasant. It is only when the emotions are impersonalized, they are transformed into rasa and give aesthetic delight. This is called *sadharanikarana* or generalizing of emotions. *Soka* (grief) has been transformed into karuna rasa (compassion) in this *Sloka* (verse). Being transcended into rasa, the sting of grief attached to it has been removed so that it can now be enjoyed and shared by the whole humanity. The escape from personal grief and its transcendence to a universal phenomenon gives the verse its aesthetic delight. The Sanskrit theorists thus anticipate what Eliot is trying to say about impersonality in art.

Paul Valery holds that the poet himself does not undergo any personal emotion in the poetic sense: that is, the poet does

---

52 Ingall 117. (*Locana* 1: 5 A)..

53 Ingall 118.

not experience the poetic state; he has to create it in others. Even this extreme view is reminiscent of Abhinavagupta.

For Abhinavagupta, the aesthetic enjoyment in the reader follows aesthetic object (text). Poetic semantics culminates in rasa. And rasa is always suggested, according to Anandavardhana. The suggestive mode, then, is essentially a presentational mode, not discursive.

It is interesting to note that Anandavardhana enlarged the term "meaning" by including all that is conveyed by a poem. There is the usual lexical meaning, the syntactic meaning and the metaphorical meaning. There is, however, a fourth order of meaning and it is the suggested meaning which enhances the value of a literary work because this brings about the realization of rasa.

Dhvani operates in terms of larger unities and not just at the level of the individual words because it explains the emotive, cognitive and socio-cultural meanings. The multiple meanings are unified and integrated into a rich and complex whole. Dhvani theory integrates what Philip Wheelwright calls "plurisignation" where the expressive language carries multiple meanings. As the Chinese saying goes, "The sound stops short, the sense flows on."[54] Dhvani is thus the outcome of the entire context of the poetic situation and by bringing in the element of rasa it anticipates the New Critical concerns of the concept of poetic language.

54 Lawrence Binyon, *Painting in the Far East* (New York: Dover, 1959), p.158.

3

The Stylistics of Deviance in Kuntaka's *Vakroktijivita*

Kuntaka lays down briefly that his object in writing a fresh treatise on poetics, when many others already exist in the field, is "to establish the idea of strikingness which causes extraordinary charm in poetry."[55] The phrase, "strikingness," characterizing the concept of vakrokti is the central principle of his poetic theory. For vakrokti, which he maintains is essential to poetry, is taken as a kind of *victra abhidha* (striking denotation) so that the vakra-bhava (obliquity) underlying it becomes synonymous with *vaicitrya* (strikingness).

The *vakrata* includes a strikingness of expression which is different from the one found in the established mode of speech in the *sastras* and scientific treatises. It is, therefore, a deviation from the general usage of language. Kuntaka explains vakrokti as an idea expressed with a view to attaining strikingness of poetic effect.

Referring to the conventional view that the alliance of the word and its sense constitutes poetry, Kuntaka lays down the special qualifications of this alliance in the use of the figure of "vakrokti." He does not agree with Dandin that a mere word or idea may be charming; what really makes the alliance poetic, according to him, is the srikingness of vakrokti.

55 Kuntaka, *Vakroktijivita,* trans. K. Krishnamoorthy (Dharwad: Karanataka University, 1977), pp. I.2, 288.

Kuntaka, however, did not put enough emphasis on rasa (aesthetic element) and bhava (emotion) as elements of poetry. Although he admits the necessity of rasa, he regards its delineation apparently as a special way of realizing obliquity in a composition. He seems to agree with Anandavardhana that it is not the mere matter but the beauty imparted to it by the continuous development of rasa which makes poetry alive. He, however, remarks that rasa could be comprehended only as an element of vakrokti.

Unlike Bhamaha and Dandin, he did not give rasa the status of a mere figure of speech. By his time, Anandavardhana had already worked out the importance of rasa and indicated its position as an essential element in poetry. So Kuntaka had to assign a more definite place to rasa in his poetic theory than merely placing it as a figure of speech.

While discussing the notion of vakya-vakrata (sentential obliquity) in which the svabhava (nature) of an object forms the theme, Kuntaka gives directions as to how sentient objects can be described and made attractive through the proper development of the sentiments. He recognizes the importance of rasa in poetry and allows it to be a constitutive element in the two kinds of style, the sukumara (delicate or soft style) and the vicitra (striking style). Kuntaka belongs to that group of authors after Anandavardhana's time who does not deny the concept of dhvani but tries to explain it in terms of vakrokti.

Although the concept of vakrokti is usually associated with Kuntaka, it has had a long tradition in Indian aesthetic theory. The theory of vakrokti shows a remarkable divergence of conception and treatment, developed in the works of Bhamaha, Kuntaka, Abhinavagupta, Bhoja, Rudrata and Mammata. Vakrokti literally means indirect speech. In the wider sense, it means strikingness or deviance in expression. Deviation can be of different kinds, but the most effective deviation is vakrokti.

Vakrokti is the basis of poetic language. The theory of vakrokti has emerged as a viable theory of the language of poetry. As poetry is a linguistic organization, vakrokti or obliquity is considered to be the most constitutive element of the poetic language.

Though the concept of vakrokti has been in use for a long time in ancient time by Subandhu, Amaru and Bana, a detailed treatment of it is made in Bhamaha's work. Bhamaha mentions it as a figure of speech. He owes his use of the concept to Bharata's *Natyasastra,* where Bharata refers to vakrokti in the context of defining laksanas (secondary meaning). Bharata devotes four chapters to what he calls *vacika-abhinaya* (linguistic representation) where he discusses in detail diction, rules on the use of language, modes of address and intonation, and styles. He emphasizes laksanas and their significance in poetry. He also refers to obliquity as secondary meaning, which has similar properties to those of vakrokti. Laksana, according to Bharata, is the essence of all poetic figures and lends strikingness to poetry.

Laksanas are a set of beautifying factors and are also called vibhusanas. Abhinavagupta defines laksanas as those beautiful elements: "which impart such pleasing turns by the poetic expression and look different from the ordinary."[56] Laksanas, which look like alamkaras or mere turn of expressions, are in fact manifestations of strikingness of speech and benefactors of figures of speech.

Bharata regards other poetic elements subordinate to laksanas. Laksanas are endowed with a natural grace and originate from the poet's imagination and make poetry more acceptable even other embellishments. Their presence adds to the charm of the figures.

---

56 Abhinavagupta, *Abhinavabharati,* ed. Ramakrishna Kavi (Poona: Bhandrarkar Oriental Institute, 1956),. pp. i-iv.

Abhinavagupta compares the different stages in the production of poetry to those in building a house. Lakshanas are like the construction of walls; the use of alamkaras is like adorning the walls with paintings. Alamkaras exist apart from what the object of presentation is; they are like a garland in poetry which is apart from the body but serves to beautify it. Laksanas are, on the other hand, beautiful characteristics of the body itself.

Abhinavagupta's analysis reveals that Bharata's laksanas are akin to what Bhamaha designates as vakrokti. P.C. Lahiri quotes S.P. Bhattacharya who remarked that Bharata's laksanas are "much more than a poetic element like guna and alamkara," and that they "might well be taken as an elastic poetic principle" which, like Kuntaka's *vakrokti,* includes within its scope other poetic elemtents."[57]

Abhinavagupta, too, is of the view that there is no distinction between laksanas and vakrokti. It seems reasonable to believe that the vakrokti of Bhamaha was foreshadowed in Bharata's laksanas.

Abhinavagupta equates obliquity with a "consummate composition" which is a generic quality found in all figures. He remarks:

> *There is, in fact, the strikingness in words and meanings and it consists in their transgressing the ordinary. This very quality characterises poetic figures, and it is a heightened form of expression that distinguishes poetic speech from the matter-of-fact speech of everyday life. Atisayokti is found in all figures.*[58]

The concept of vakrokti has had a "chequered career" in Indian poetics. It has had conspicuous ups and downs. Even some modern scholars have considered vakrokti to be one of the

---

57 P. C. Lahiri, *Concept of Riti and Guna in Sanskrit Poetics* (Delhi: V.K. Publishing House, 1987), p.17.

58 Abhinavagupta iv.

"byways" of Sanskrit criticism which could be connected and linked up with the highways of literary criticism like rasa and dhvani. The theory of vakrokti has long been neglected since the time of Kuntaka.

Kuntaka had given vakrokti the most elaborate treatment. He deals with it in the very detailed way, delineating its nature, types and significance in poetry.

He has given vakrokti a full fledged theory of poetic expression. To him, vakrokti is synonymous with poetry (kavya) itself. Both inadequate expression and expression devoid of idea are, according to him, of no use. He calls a beautiful expression without a beautiful idea "dead" (*mrtakalpa*) and a beautiful idea expressed in not an equally beautiful form as "diseased" (vyadhibhuta). He defines poetry in three ways: poetry is the poet's achievement; poetry consists in ornamentation; poetry is the mingling of sound and sense, which is established in a composition embodying the poetic activity of a deviational character. The third definition of poetry is a logical development of the other two.

According to Kuntaka, poetry is an alliance of word and its meaning. He remarks:

> *Poetry is a coalescence of sound and sense which is established in a composition embodying the poetic activity of a deviational character, and which delights those who know the true nature of poetry.*[59]

Explaining his theoretical position he further remarks:

> *Both words and meanings are to be embellished and their embellishment lies in their obliqueness. Vakrokti is an ingenious utterance peculiar to poetry and is distinct from popular usage. It is a clever turn of speech, witty and startling in effect.*[60]

---

59 Kuntaka I.7 292.

60 Kuntaka I.8 300.

But this alliance of sound and sense must have the speciality of being characterized by vakrata or vaicitrya (obliquity). Dandin had maintained that poetry is embellishment of words communicating the desired meaning. Kuntaka disagrees with Dandin that mere word, however charming it may be, or mere idea conveyed by it, does not constitute poetry; what makes them poetic is the presence of the striking quality of obliquity.

The role of the poet in poetic expression is very important because it is the poet's act of imagination that gives the expression its desired obliquity. By recognizing the significance of the poet's imagination in poetic creation, Kuntaka has established the theory of vakrokti on a firm aesthetic footing.

According to Kuntaka, obliquity is an essential factor in poetry which depends upon the individual power of the poet. It helps poetry impart an unspeakable delight to the connoisseur because it distinguishes poetry from matter-of-fact speech. Kuntaka believes that poetry becomes lively in association with vakrokti.

Vakrokti is a functional element of poetry (Kavi-Vyapara-Vakratra). It is also recognized as the embellishment (alamkrti) of the word and its meaning, the physical constituents to poetry. Kuntaka says that an unembellished poetry can hardly be conceived. He believes that poetic delectableness causes an elevation of spirit; he thinks that whatever renders poetry charming must be recognized as vakrokti.

Bhoja has also discussed vakrokti in his work. He used the term in three different senses: the poetic expression in general, the figure of speech beginning with upama (simile), and one of the varieties of the verbal figure called vakovakya. Bhoja does not use vakrokti in its large sense frequently. There is, however, some similarity between Bhoja's and Kuntaka's concepts of vakrokti. Bhoja defines poetry as opposed to non-oblique language used in scientific treatise and other common discourses.

Bhoja thus defines poetry in terms of vakrokti. He designates vakrokti as an extraordinary, rounded expression (visista- bhaniti). At times he see Blackmur ms to be working out a reconciliation between *dhvani* and *vakrokti.* While assigning to dhvani a supreme position in poetry, he at the same time emphasizes the significance of vakrokti without which, he feels, poetry will be a mere speech.

Though Kuntaka's concept of vakrokti was not endorsed by later writers, his views regarding strikingness as the central characteristic of the language of poetry were widely accepted. Ruyyaka, for example, regarded a poetic figure as a particular form of speech. Commenting on the figure anumana (inference), he affirmed that it cannot be distinguished from the logician's inference unless there is a particular strikingness depending on the sense.[61] Mammata also believes that the charm of expression can come out of figures even where there is no rasa. He goes to the extent of maintaining that a figure is nothing else than strikingness itself. To him a hyperbolical expression constitutes the main ingredient of poetry.[62] The views of Panditaraja Jagannatha are clearer still. He too looks upon a figure as a specialized expression and holds strkingness to be the generic trait of all figures. This strikingness, he says, results from the charm brought about by the poet's imagination.[63]

Strikingness serves as the essence for all poetic expression. The element of wonder that results from strikingness is an invariable part of poetic enjoyment. The idea regarding strikingness of poetic expression has kept on appearing variously in Indian poetics. It emerged in the form of Bharata's "laksana," Vamana's "bandha-gumpha," Anandavardhana's

61 Ruyyaka, *Alamkarasarvasva,* ed. Girijaprasad Dvivedi (Bombay: Nirnaya Sagar Press, 1939), pp. 148-49.

62 Mammata, *Kavyaprakasa,* ed. Sivaprasad Bhattacharya (Calcutta: Sanskrit College, 1961), p. 301.

63 Jagannatha, *Rasagangadhara,* ed. Badrinath Jha and M.M.Jha (Varanasi: Chowkhamba Sanskrit Series, 1955), p..203.

"bandhacchaya" and "uktivaicitrya" and Rajasekhara's "bhaniti-vaicitrya." These ideas were present in these writers in a disorganised form, but it was left to Kuntaka to treat them in a systematic and comprehensive way.

Kuntaka, however, is fully convinced that it is the expressional deviation or strikingness that is the most important element, which is responsible for the effectiveness and charm in poetry. In his prologue to *Karpuramanjari,* Rajasekhara also maintains that neither the idea, nor the word, but the manner of expressing the idea in words makes poetry worth reading. Kuntaka is even more categorical. He cannot imagine a position in which poetry can be seen dissociated from its figures. He has variously affirmed the essentiality of poetic obliquity. A strikingness in speech, he maintains, imparts an excellent charm even to an object which is stale and tasteless.

Oblique speech, for Kuntaka, is the general principle underlying all figures of speech. The comprehensiveness of Kuntaka's concept of vakrokti can be measured from an analysis of his treatment of the "sukumara marg" (brilliant style). To him, vakrokti is the only embellishment possible to the word and its meaning. Both the word and meaning are adorned and their adornment consists in the poetic process known as vakrokti. He, thus comments:

> *Word and meaning have their distinct existence in poetry and come to be adorned by something different from themselves. The fact is that the very process of poetic utterance is constituted by oblique turns assumed by words and meanings. The poetic process itself, in this sense, is the real ornamentation and is extremely delighting.*[64]

Kuntaka never thought of poetry in a purely formalistic, mechanical way and in terms of its drab technicalities. He remarks:

64 Kuntaka I.10 306-307.

> *Just as the excellence of a painting transcends the beauty of various shades and colours on the canvas, the poet's art far excels the beauty, of individual elements such as words, meanings, attributes and figures.*[65]

His concept of vakrokti may not have been developed from Manoratha's verse where vakrokti means only an excellent arrangement of words. He probably took cue from Avantisundari, but developed and established the concept in a profoundly fresh way.

However, his theory has been occasionally subjected to criticism. His theory of poetry, Lahiri says, "lacks precision. Kuntaka has spared no pains to form a definite and unique theory of poetry... but his theory has remained indefinite to his readers." Lahiri attributes this indefiniteness to Kuntaka's comprehensiveness, "grandiloquent expressions and large generalization."[66] S.P. Bhattacharya believes that Kuntaka possessed "the state of a genuine critic but not the dash of a genius."[67] Vijayavardhana criticises Kuntaka's theory of poetry as "far-fetched and unrealistic" and "rather strained," which "tried to explain poetry mainly from the formal point of view.[68]

Most of these commentators, however, tend to forget Kuntaka's objectives and look at his theory from a rather narrow point of view. Despite these criticisms, Kuntaka has been hailed as "one of the rare original minds of later Indian poetics who attempted to account for poetry in terms of the essentially non-literal character."[69] His sturdy independence prompted him to formulate a new theory of poetics without adhering to the

---

65 Kuntaka III.4 419.

66 P.C. Lahiri 147.

67 S.P. Bhattacharya, *Studies in Indian Poetics* (Calcutta: Firma KLM Pvt. Ltd., 1964), p.116.

68 G.Vijayavardhana, *Outlines of Sanskrit Poetics* (Varanasi: Chowkhamba Sanskrit Series, 1970), pp. 131,135.

69 Lahiri 148.

teachings of the orthodox scholars. Krishnamoorthy comments on the value of Kuntaka's theory:

> *Whoever understands Kuntaka's varkrokti narrowly to mean an oblique trope, as understood by say Rudrata, would be doing a gross injustice to his freshness of thought... "vakrokti" of Kuntaka is a synonym for the principle of beauty underlying the poetic language as such.*[70]

Poetry, says Kuntaka, is the activity of the poet, which produces transcendental delight in responsive readers. He devotes nearly the whole of his *Vakroktijivita*, with the exception of the introductory portion of his first chapter, to the definition, classification and illustration of six varieties of vakrokti. These varieties operate at six levels of poetic expression: phonetic, lexical, grammatical, sentential, contextual, and the composition as a whole. Taken together they represent, in fact, inter-linked categories characterising the nature of speech. Kuntaka elaborates:

> *Obliquity is of six types each with a number of sub-divisions, each subdivision striking the reader by a subtle nuance of poetry. The six types are: obliquity in the arrangement of syllables; obliquity in the base forms of substantives; obliquity in the whole sentence admitting of a thousand varieties, including a whole lot of figures; obliquity in parts or incidents; obliquity in the entire composition, which may be spontaneous or studied, both transmitting beauty and delight.*[71]

The second chapter of his book takes up for detailed consideration the first three varieties of vakrokti. The third chapter deals with vakyavakrata and the fourth prakaranavakrakta and prabandhavakrata. Thus the entire book deals in a comprehensive manner the ubiquitous presence of vakrokti in poetic language.

---

70 K. Krishnamoorthy, *Studies in Indian Aesthetics and Criticism* (Mysore: D.V.K. Murthy, 1979), pp. 190-91.

71 Kuntaka I.18-21 389-92.

Kuntaka has recognized in the arrangement of syllables of phonetic obliquity the first variety of vakrokti. He seems to regard phonemes as the foremost basis of analysis of poetry. This type of vakrokti, which relies upon the arrangements of consonants, is known as alliteration. This type includes, besides the use of alliteration, also the more subtle sound effects produced by the free and irregular repetition of similar or identical phonemes at varying intervals. Kuntaka remarks:

> *Sometimes alliteration without any interval too, employed artistically by the poet, contributes to high poetic charm because of variation in vowels, when alliteration is effected without extra effort, when it is adorned with syllables which are not harsh, when it becomes appealing by discontinuance of earlier sound repetitions and by new choices for reiteration.*[72]

These effects are of great importance in determining the precise nature of attributes and styles based on them. Kuntaka is, however, fully aware of the limitations of this kind of obliquity. Alliteration, he holds, should never violate propriety and should be in consonance with the feelings conveyed. Moreover, they should be very carefully chosen and should not be tarnished by unattractive phonemes. The poets can make their work more beautiful by the repetition of novel phonemes. And finally, lucidity should always be maintained.

The second type, lexical obliquity, comprises all effects based on the choice and use of words. This can have various forms. When a word in common usage, Kuntaka writes, is used so as to include an attribution of associative meanings other than the primary meaning, we have an example of lexical obliquity.

Another instance of lexical obliquity is the use of synonyms in an artistic way. Usage has conferred certain properties and associations on words, and synonyms have different shades of

72 Kuntaka II-4 365.

meaning and distinct associations. The most important kind of this variety of obliquity is due to transference (upacara) when a word is used in a secondary sense to refer to an object with which it is not directly associated. Kuntaka comments thus:

> *When the stated and the implied, though apparently far removed from each other, have a common attribute, however slight, which lends itself to hyperbolic treatment and adds charm and delight to figures of speech like metaphor, we have obliquity of metaphorical expression.*[73]

This variety also includes such devices as speaking of an abstract phenomenon as it was some material which could be handled as if it is animate.

Another important sub-variety of this kind of vakrokti is called obliquity of usage. Kuntaka thus remarks on this:

> *When a conventional denotation of words inheres connotation of even improbable meanings or includes exaggeration of an attribute in the poet's attempt to express extrordinary derision or supreme exaltation of the object, we have obliquity in the infinitude of usage.*[74]

Obliqiuty of epithet is yet another sub-variety of lexical obliquity. "If the excellence of an epithet," Kuntaka says, "heightens the beauty of a verb or substantive, we have obliquity of epithet."[75]

Kuntaka is fully conscious of poetic beauty arising out of these components. He has also dealt with certain other sub-varieties of lexical obliquity. Obliquity of concealment (Samvrti) operates when the subject of description is screened by the use of pronouns and so on for achieving excellence of expression. This is associated with the poet's keenness to convey the infinite speciality of the object being described.

73 Kuntaka II.13-14 381.

74 Kuntaka II.8-9 369-370.

75 Kuntaka II.10 373.

Obliquity in the use of affixes adds to the beauty of decorum in the subject described by making for a striking originality in a composition. The other sub-varieties which Kuntaka mentioned are: obliquity in adverbial, "root activity" (bhava) and gender. There is one more sub-variety of this kind, the one pertaining to the speciality of verbs, which can be realized in five forms:

> *Obliquity of verbal forms is seen when there is cohesion of the subject with the verbs, when another subject attains excellence in relation to the same verb, when the adverbials go to qualify it, when metaphorical superimposition heightens the beauty of the verb form and when the direct object, though concealed, gets charmingly communicated.*[76]

In a poetic composition, Kuntaka adds, the poet is also guided by considerations of special tense, case, number, person, preposition, particles, and so on. He discusses these various sources in his treatment of obliquity in the inflectional forms of substantives. This variety of obliquity may also be called grammatical obliquity. It includes all possibilities of grammatical construction of an expression. Anandavardhana has included most of these sub-varieties in his treatment of dhvani.

Kuntaka concludes his discussion by maintaining that "when several forms of literary turns occur together in such a way as to enhance the beauty of one another, they produce artistic charm reminiscent of myriad-faced beauty."[77] The poetic speech, to him, is a creeper, with words as leaves, which give striking beauty to expression while enriching our feelings and rasas.

The next variety of vakrokti operates at the level of sentence. Kuntaka says:

---

76 Kuntaka II 24-25 395.

77 Kuntaka II.34 408.

Obliquity of sentence is distinct from the richness of beauty born of attributes and figures in so far as they relate to artistic words and content expressed in varied styles. In fact, expressiveness of the sentence form should be regarded as the essence of this beauty. Just as the excellence of a painting transcends the beauty of various shades and colours on canvas, the poet's art far excels the beauty of individual elements such as word, meaning, attributes and embellishments.[78]

Obliquity in sentence has a thousand varieties including the whole range of figures of speech. Kuntaka follows the list of figures given by Bhamaha but revises it by redefining the figures to lend greater precision to his analysis.

Kuntaka, unlike Bhamaha, distinguishes figures from subject matter. But he accepts only eighteen figures. He remarks that the other figures, which he does not include, are either not different from the figures listed or lack aesthetic charm. A sentence, for him, is nothing but an assemblage of many beautifying elements. Comparing the strikingness of a sentence with that of a charming woman, he remarks:

A good poet's oblique speech appeals to one's heart even like one's beloved. Both the beloved and poetic speech share common features, i.e., striking graceful qualities, alluring charm of word usage or foot-steps, elegant but sparse ornaments, tasteful sentiment, tender-heartedness and elegance of expression.[79]

He also discusses obliquity of subject matter. He says: "When the subject matter is described in a way conducive to beauty by virtue of its own infinite natural charm and by means of exclusively artistic expresions, we have an example

78 Kuntaka III. 3-4 419.

79 Kuntaka III.64 535.

of creative beauty relating to content."[80] Content which is beautiful serves an integral purpose in a poetic composition. The subject matter may be "natural" (sahaja) or "imposed" (aharya) by the poet. When the subject-matter, Kuntaka implies, is naturally beautiful, it does not have to be heavily embellished.

The senence is no longer regarded as the largest unit of linguistic analysis. The concept of "discourse" has opened up possibilities of the analysis of a text from a wider-than-sentence perspective. It is remarkable that Kuntaka does not finish off his analysis at the level of sentence but deals with obliquity in terms of the context and the entire composition. When the intended object is capable of maintaining a sense of unpredictability and is "the product of the unique, boundless poetic skill underlying it, we have the obliquity of episode or incident."[81]

Kuntaka also describes ten sub-varieties of the obliquity of episode. If the results are excellent, he does not care for the rules. He says, "It should not be vitiated by an excessive craze for observing rules even when they (*chandhas*) are inopportune, provided the episode reveals a unique charm of originality." So what he values most in the use of episodes is an organic unity. He goes on to say:

> *An organic unity which strikingly underlies various incidents described in different parts of the work leading to intended end, each bound to the other by a relationship of mutual assistance, reveals the essence of creative originality which is most delectable in the case of rare poetic geniuses who are endowed with the gift of an extraordinary creative imagination.*[82]

80 Kuntaka III.1 411.

81 Kuntaka IV.2 537.

82 Kuntaka IV.15 566.

The last variety he discusses is the obliquity of composition itself. This type of vakrokti, he claims, has the beauty of the combined effect of the other five varieties. At this point Kuntaka's text is fragmentary. He describes seven main sub-varieties of the obliquity of the entire composition.

According to him, the poet may change the rasa of the source story to make his work delightful; he may make only one part of the original story the subject matter of his work. The very title of the work may possess strikingness indicating the tilt being given to it; an abbreviated story may be expanded or an extensive one cut short by the author. Finally, the whole work of the author may be oblique, giving instructions and telling new ways of success. Even if poets use an identical theme for their literary works, they use it so differently that each work has its own inherent beauty.

Kuntaka's treatment of the six varieties of vakrokti along with their sub-varieties is very detailed and impressive. Krishnamoorthy comments on this aspect thus: "Kuntaka had tried to widen the application of the idea of vakrokti so as to include all types of *camatkara* in poetry. And his classification of several varieties of *vakrokti* was no doubt ingenious but hardly serviceable."[83]

Kuntaka tried to establish the supremacy of vakrokti in poetry as Anandavardhana did for dhvani. His classification is more scientific than Anandavardhana's: beginning with the minimal unit of sound, i.e., phonemes, he goes on to describe vakrokti at the level of a composite, extensive unit of discourse, i.e., *mahakavya*. In his efforts to make his classification comprehensive, he equates some of the varieties of vakrokti with those of dhvani. Some of Kuntaka's contemporaries believed that Kuntaka's theory of vakrokti was nothing other than the theory of dhvani in disguise.

---

83 K. Krishnamoorthy, *Dhvanyaloka and Its Critics* (Mysore: Kavyalaya Pub., 1966), p. 306.

Kuntaka, as Warder points out, was "no doubt inspired by Bhartṛhari's similar conception of language as indivisible utterances or sentences, grammatical analysis being only abstraction and not a discovery of real roots, suffixes, etc."[84]

II

The two kinds of poetry which Tillyard discusses are "direct" and "oblique." The concept of oblique poetry has not been clearly formulated by Western scholars, nor have they applied it to critical practice, as has been done by the Indian poeticians. Aristotle was the first Western scholar to accept the full significance of obliquity in poetry. He regards metaphor as the greatest thing in poetry, the "mark of genius." As he says, "It is one thing that cannot be learnt from others; and it is also a sign of genius, since good metaphor implies an intuitive perception of the similarity in dissimilarity."[85]

In the Graeco-Roman tradition no critic has been so seriously concerned with obliquity as Longinus. According to him. "The effect of elevated language upon an audience is not persuasion but transport."[86] He explains in detail the structure of speech and all the devices that lead to the sublime. He remarks:

> *The sublime consists in a certain loftiness and consummateness of language, and it is by this and this only that the greatest poets and prose writers have won pre-eminence and lasting fame.*[87]

He goes on to say that in poetry "we look for something transcending the human, the extraordinary, the great and

---

84 A.K. Warder, *Indian Kavya Literature. vol. I* (Delhi: Motilal Banarasidass, 1972), p. 106.

85 Aristotle, *Poetics*, trans. Ingram Bywater in *The Basic Works of Aristotle*, ed. Richard McKeon (New York: Random House, 1941), p. 1459a.

86 Longinus, *On the Sublime*, ed. T.S. Dorsch (London: Penguin, 1969), p. 100.

87 Longinus 100.

the beautiful."[88] Croce designates artistic beauty in poetry as a "verbal paradox." To him "the aesthetic fact... is form, and nothing but form." He remarks:

> *Language is a perpetual creation. What has been linguistically expressed in not repeated, save by reproduction of what has already been reproduced. The ever-new impressions give rise to continuous changes of sound and meaning, that is, to ever-new expressions. To seek the model language is to seek the immobility of motion.*[89]

There is a remarkable similarity between vakrokti and some of the tenets of Russian Formalism and New Criticism. The New Critics consider the arrangement or form of a poem as the most important matter, to them form is the basis of the intensity of poetry. They equate form with meaning; the aesthetics of organicism has been a major preoccupation with them. According to Cleanth Brooks, "The most critical discoveries of our time—perhaps if not a discovery but merely a recovery—is that the parts of a poem have an organic relation to each other."[90]

The New Critics analysed poems in terms of opposites like texture/structure, extension/intention etc, and this critical practice is determined by the "principle of variety in unity or the reconciliation of the opposites." The analysis takes into account the technical principles of ambiguity, polysemy, paradox and irony and such other features. Vakrokti is thus analogous to these concepts of New Criticism.

William Empson used the term "ambiguity" to refer to words and sentences with secondary meanings. His *Seven Types of Ambiguity* is instrumental in highlighting the importance of this trope implying the dynamics of poetic meaning. Wimsatt

88 Longinus 148.

89 Benetto Croce, *Aesthetic* (London: Oxford UP, 1922), p.253.

90 Cleanth Brooks and R.P. Warren, *Understanding Poetry* (New York: Henry Holt, 1938), p.71.

and Brooks refer to Empson's book as having "brought home to a whole generation of readers the fact of the many-sidedness of language."[91] It is the ambiguity that enables the poet to meet the double demand made of the language of poetry. Empson's treatment of ambiguity is similar to I.A. Richards'. The poet, according to Richards, has to make inexpressibly complex adjustment and hence his ambiguity:

> *The natural generality and vagueness of all references which is not made specific by the aid of space and time is of great importance for the understanding of the senses in which poetry may be said to be true.*[92]

Richards talks of "the state-of-order-disorder within our lexical structural would-be system called poetry."[93] "Poetry with insides," Richards continues, "gives most pleasure when only generally...understood."[94] Richards sees ambiguity as nothing abnormal. He equates the study of poetry with the study of the modes of language, characterized by "the ambiguities and confusions that are overt or latent."[95] He also points out that ambiguity, which exists everywhere, is in particular "the indispensable means of most of our important utterance—especially in poetry and religion.[96]

The poetic language occasions multiple interpretations. In *The Meaning of Meaning*, Richards calls poetry the supreme form

---

91 W.K. Wimsatt and Cleanth Brooks, *Literary Criticism: A Short History* (London: Routledge, 1957), p.638.

92 I.A. Richards, *Principles of Literary Criticism* (London: Routledge and Kegan Paul, 1948), p.160.

93 I.A. Richards, "The Future of Poetry," *The Screens and Other Poems* (New York: Norton, 1960), p.126.

94 I.A. Richards, *Coleridge on Imagination* (London: Routledge and Kegan Paul, 1962), p.214.

95 I.A. Richards, *Coleridge on Imagination*, p. 232.

96 I.A. Richards, *The Philoshphy of Rhetoric* (London: Oxford UP, 1936), p. 40.

of emotive language. The language of poetry, as against the non-poetic language, is "fluid." He goes on to explain this fluidity:

> *There is an important use of words... (in poetry) which does not freeze its meanings but leaves them fluid, which does not fix an assertorial clip upon them in the way that scientific prose and factual discourse must. It leaves them to move about and relate themselves in various ways to one another.*[97]

It is this "fluidity" of meaning that gives abiding charm to poetry. Ambiguity, in the sense of multiple implications, is a natural, subtle and effective instrument for poetry and dramatic purposes. On this account, poetic language means all it says and suggests even what it does not say.

Ransom points out that the concreteness of poetry does not prevent it from becoming ambiguous. If the artist has an observant mind, his compositions are likely to be rich and suggestive. The distinguishing feature of poetry is ambiguity which does not only mean having a double meaning. Therefore, devices like pun do not constitute ambiguity, because there is no scope for "puzzlement" here. The kind of ambiguity that Empson talks of originates from extensions of meaning from either a single word or juxtaposition of words; ambiguity is always bound up with figure and imagery.

The seven types of ambiguity mentioned by Empson are types of "logical disorder" in order of increasing distance from simple statement and logical exposition. These seven types are kinds in which:

> *a detail is effective in several ways at once; two or more alternative meanings are fully resolved into one; two apparently unconnected meanings are given simulaneously; alternative meanings combine to make a complicated state of mind in the author; a fortunate confusion is present which*

---

97 I.A. Richards, *Speculative Instruments* (Chicago: University of Chicago Press, 1955), p.148.

owes its inception to the author's discovering his idea in the act of writing or not holding it all in his mind at once, what is said is contradictory or irrelevant and the reader is forced to invent interpretations; and full contradiction is in operation marking a division in the author's mind.[98]

Brooks defines poetry in terms of structure. This structure is far more internal than the metrical pattern or the sequence of images; it is "a structure of meanings, evaluations and interpretation," and the principle of unity which informs it seems to be one of "balancing and harmonising connotations, attitudes and meanings."[99] Such a structure involves irony and paradox. The "prose-sense" fails to represent the inner, essential or real structure of the poem.

"Irony," according to Brooks, is "the kind of qualification which the various elements in a content receive from the context." It is the "recognition of incongruities."[100] Brooks' irony, in other words, refers to a poetic device which involves "the less extreme kinds of modification of a word by its context."[101]

Brooks' concepts of "irony" and "paradox" are interlinked. He thinks poetry in terms of paradox, which is structural. He regards paradox as "a device for contrasting the conventional views of a situation, or the limited and special view of it such as those taken in practical and scientific discourse, with a more inclusive view."[102] He believes that almost all great poems ensure the presence of irony and paradox. He maintains that "paradox is the language appropriate and inevitable to poetry" and that poetry is different from the scientist's language which

98 William Empson, *Seven Types of Ambiguity* (London: Penguin, 1947), pp. v-vi.

99 Cleanth Brooks *The Well-Wrought Urn* (New York: Harcourt, Brace & Co., 1947), pp. 178-79.

100 Cleanth Brooks 191.

101 Brooks and Warren 587.

102 Cleanth Brooks 230.

is "purged of every trace of paradox." He further remarks in his essay "The Language of Paradox" that, "...the paradox springs from the very nature of the poet's language."[103] Even a "simple and straightforward poet is forced into paradoxes by the nature of his instrument."[104] The poets consciously employ paradox to gain compression and precision. The method, says Brooks, "is an extension of the normal language of poetry, [and] not a perversion of it."[105]

Brooks has been criticized for his critical monism. While acknowledging his "valuable contributions," Crane criticizes Brooks for presenting a theory which has a "fundamental error" in it:

> *...he has begun to theorize about poetry at the wrong end—starting not with concrete poetic wholes of various kinds, the parts of which with their possible interrelationships, can be inferred as consequences from inductively established principles, but rather with one only of the several internal causes of poems, and the cause which they have most common with all other literary productions, namely, their linguistic matter: here he begins, and here also he ends. The choice is regrettable, since it prevents him from dealing adequately with poetic works in terms of the sufficient or distinguishing causes of their production and nature...*[106]

Despite frequent occurrences of the terms "irony" and "paradox" in his works, Brooks himself admits that perhaps they are inadequate and misleading."[107]

103 Cleanth Brooks 8.

104 Cleanth Brooks 9.

105 Cleanth Brooks 10.

106 R.S. Crane, "The Critical Monism of Cleanth Brooks," in *Critics and Criticism*, ed. R. S. Crane (Toronto: Univ of Tornoto Press, 1953), p. 105.

107 Cleanth Brooks 179.

Allen Tate describes poetry in terms of tension. The poet, according to him, "has an immediate responsibility... for the vitality of language"; his task is the preservation of "the integrity, the purity, and the reality of language."[108] The poet has an edge over the scientist, for his inner field of experience is denied to the latter, and he has the resources of figurative language at his disposal.[109] Tate believes that a poet is known by his language and not by his subject matter: "For in the long run, whatever the poet's 'philosophy', however wide may be the extension of his meaning . . . by his language shall you know him; the quality of his language is the valid limit of what he has to say."[110] The quality of a poem can be determined by its total effect, to examine which one has its configuration of meaning. "The meaning of poetry," says Tate, " is the 'tension', the full organized body of all the extension and intension that we can find in it."[111] "Extension," as logicians use the word, stands for denotation, and "intention," for connotation. In the ordinary or logical use of the term, the two are of inverse relationship. A poem is a verbal structure which in some peculiar way has both a wide "extension" and a deep "intention." All good poetry, Tate maintains, is "a unity of all the meanings from the furthest extremes of intention and extension," and the recognition of these meaning is "the gift of experience."[112]

These views have a striking parallel with those of Kuntaka's. Kuntaka defines literature at one point as the mutual tension, or rivalry of word and meaning. His is a theory of poetic tension of general validity, in which tension is compatible with basic harmony, as is evident from his definition of literature as the coexistence of sound and sense. Kuntaka, however, extends

108 Allen Tate, *The Man of Letters in the Modern World* (New York: Harcourt, 1955), pp. 11, 20.

109 Allen Tate 35.

110 Allen Tate 73.

111 Allen Tate 71.

112 Allen Tate 70.

his concept from the poetic moment to the poetic continuum. The parity of sound and meaning, the notion of a "jealousy" between them, and the sub-ordination of the two to the total poetic expression are the most important features of the concept of tension in poetry.

Another concept that bears obvious resemblances to vakrokti is Blackmur's theory of language as "gesture." "When the language of words fail," Blackmur writes, "we resort to the language of gesture."[113] The language cannot be put to its highest use without incorporating within it some such quality of gesture. He further observes,

> *Nor can we master language purposefully without re-mastering gesture within it. Gesture in language is the outward and dramatic play of inward and imaged meaning. It is that play of meaningfulness among words which cannot be defined in the formulas in the dictionary... gesture is that meaningfulness which is moving, in every sense of that word: what moves the words and what moves us.*[114]

Gesture, Blackmur claims, is of great structural importance in poetry. It is "native" to language, without which language would get dry and petrified. It comes before language, but when it goes with language, the language is animated by it. Blackmur regards gesture as "what objectively joins the perceptions of the different senses together, heightening them into a single sensation."[115]

Blackmur's concept of "gesture" can be placed alongside the Indian concepts of dhvani and vakrokti. Blackmur draws a distinction between the "language of silence," understood by processes of mystical or intuitive knowing, and the "rational" language.

---

113 R.P. Blackmur, *Language as Gesture* (New York: Columbia UP, 1954), p.3.

114 R.P. Blackmur, 6.

115 R.P. Blackmur, 16-17.

He, however, believes that "technique" should not be confined to the linguistic arrangement in a poem, but involves the other possibilities of language for its illumination ranging from structure and tropes to sources and influences. He dislikes poetry that is unintelligible. He says:

> *True meaning... can only exist where some contact, however remote, is preserved between the language, forms, or symbols in which it is given and something concrete, individual, or sensual which inspired it, and the degree in which the meaning is seized will depend on the degree in which the particular concreteness is realized.*[116]

But the New Critics' approach to the poetic language is too circumscribed and prescriptive compared to the dynamics of vakrokti. Their assumptions, as Wimsatt points out, "have been developing in a way that makes it now difficult to speak well of poetry."[117] It is significant to note that Blackmur himself admits that the skills developed for the analysis of texts has resulted in "critical insularity."

Kuntaka has discussed six varieties of vakrokti, operating at six levels of poetic expression: phonetic, lexical, grammatical, sentential, contextual and the composition as a whole. These varieties of vakrokti can be placed beside eight kinds of deviations mentioned by Leech: lexical, grammatical, phonological, graphological, semantic, dialectical, registral, and historical deviation. In a way, Kuntaka's theory pointed towards the direction subsequent literary criticism had to take. Kuntaka regards the poet's intuition as the source of obliquity, thus giving the theory of vakrokti a human character.

Tillyard uses the word "rhythm" in a wide sense to cover all the effects that the sounds of words command. Rhythm is a powerful means of obliquity. Shelley's poem *To a Skylark*,

116 R.P. Blackmur, 396-97.

117 W.K. Wimsatt, *The Verbal Icon* (New York: University of Kentucky Press, 1954), p. 276.

Tillyard says, is an excellent example of rhythmical obliquity. The poem is not a fanciful elaboration of the skylark's song but an expression of the poet's instinctive belief in progress and achievement. The variety of rhythm in the poem suggests the elasticity of the poet's feeling. Experience proves how thoroughly the rhythm is the poem.

Another source of obliquity is symbolism. One can hardly deny the effectiveness of symbols in the poetic expression. Tillyard uses the term "symbolism" in a rather narrow sense. To him, it implies the use of certain objects as constantly significant, not subservient to other objects. It also implies the author's deliberate intention to give the objects a symbolic meaning. But Tillyard accepts symbolism as a minor form of poetical obliquity; he becomes somewhat sceptical of certain fixed symbols as they tend to become either "aridly mechanical" or "fraudulently suggestive."

Allusion, like symbolism, is regarded as a minor means of obliquity. By allusion, Tillyard means a reference, conscious or unconscious, to a passage in literature, its main function being to thicken the meaning of certain details. Allusions are helpful in attaining economy of words. They connect a poet to the tradition, and once the continuity has been established, they take on a general function. They also help the poet manipulate the "tone" of the poem.

Obliquity in a poetic composition may lend some obscurity to style, but eventually it provides density to the poetic expression. As an expressive system, poetry, particularly modern poetry, embraces all forms of obliquity as expression of deeper thought.

Oblique poetry finds expression in what has been called the "complex style." It has been pointed out that the metaphysical style of the seventeeth century English literature, the style of Browning and the difficult style of the modern poets like Hopkins are different realizations of this "complex style."

This style is marked by an unusually powerful expressiveness. Those who write in this style always attempt to say things afresh and are not afraid of boldly experimenting with new forms of expression, new tricks of style or using old techniques in new ways. The metaphysical poets, led by John Donne, shocked their contemporaries and successors by their daring innovation in language use.

Browning's is a well-known case of a poet writing obscure poetry. The sources of his poetry are his subtle and unusual themes, his varied, unfamiliar and learned allusions and illustrations, his extremely abrupt and sometimes carefree manner of putting things, all of which were part of his new technique of writing poetry. He found the conventional notion of writing inadequate and incapable of transferring his thoughts and feelings on to the dead and silent page.

Quite a few modern poets produced what could be accepted as the best specimens of oblique style. Hopkins' poetic experiments in "sprung rhythm" and "inscape" are unconventional and striking. Hopkins thought that the one aim of poetry is to grasp and express the individuality of everything in the world. An attempt to capture "inscape" in poetry will mean precision and distinctiveness in language. This would explain many apparent difficulties or "oddities" in Hopkins' vocabulary and syntax. The directness and urgency which he wishes to communicate along with his concentrated fierceness obliged him to wrench syntax, and frequently to use inversions, omissions and ellipsis. He did not use the rules of grammar, for the rules limited the possibilities of language as a medium of poetry. He was aware that his poetry may appear obscure or difficult, but had to explain to his friends that he was obscure not because he wanted to be obscure but because he could not help being obscure while striving to say quickly, minutely, powerfully and authentically what he wanted to say. It is the peculiar mode of apprehension that forces Hopkins to take recourse to the distinctive mode of saying things.

Poetry is found to be obscure when there is a breakdown in the flow of communication between the poet and his readers. But when a poet's mind is working under some kind of intense pressure, the resulting poetry gets obscure because he is raising language to a new power. "In such moments," remarks John Press, "the poet rises and falls through different levels of consciousness, leaping enormous gaps between discontinuous orders of experience, like a desperate climber... "[118]

Writing on "pure poetry," as he calls it, Valery, the French symbolist, says:

> *Every time words show a certain deviation from the most direct, that is, the most insensible expression of thought, every time deviations foreshadow, as it were, a world of relationships distinct from the purely practical world, we conceive more or less precisely, the possibility of enlarging this exceptional domain,... which, when developed and used, constitutes poetry in so far as it is an effect of art.*[119]

Valery is not aware of the danger of such a poetry. He particularly draws our attention to the "complicated and artificial" nature of the art of our age, which becomes more mysterious, narrower, more inaccessible to the people.

Mallarme has justified obsurity in poetry even more strongly:

> *Obsurity is a dangerous thing, regardless of whether it results from the reader's inadequacy or from the poet's. But if you avoid the work it involves, you are cheating... There must always be an enigma in poetry. The purpose of literature—the only purpose—is to evoke things.*[120]

---

118 John Press, *The Chequerd Shade* (London: Oxford UP, 1963), p. 191.

119 Paul Valery, *The Art of Poetry* (London: Routledge, 1958), pp.184-85.

120 Stephene Mallarme, *Mallarme: Selected Prose Poems, Essays and Letters*, trans. Bradford Cook (Baltimore: The Johns Hopkins UP, 1956), pp. 21-22.

Ambiguity arises in poetry from the poet's employment of language in a particular way to reveal several layers of meaning. Words, as Bhartṛhari says, are capable of yielding multiple meanings, even unintended ones, by force of context. Empson uses the term "ambiguity" to connote various layers of meaning in poetry. He remarks:

> *An ambiguity, in ordinary speech, means something very pronounced and as a rule witty or deceitful. I propose to use the word in an extended sense, and shall think relevant to my subject any verbal nuance, however slight, which gives room for alternative reactions to the same piece of language.*[121]

Empson's classification of ambiguities is based on their communicative effects and their contribution to the textual structure. Many of the ambiguities he deals with involve factors that cannot easily be evaluated linguistically. These levels include: levels of ability in comprehension; degrees of sensitivity and ingenuity; awareness of historical background; allegory; allusion; etymology; sound symbolism; and the poet's intentions.

Sanskrit critics have given an impressive classification of "ambiguity" on the basis of comparison (*sadharmya*), exaggeration (*atisaya*), dissimilarity (*vaisamya*), appropriateness (*aucitya*), obliqueness (*vakrokti*), and wonder (*camatkara*). Empson's seven types of ambiguity roughly correspond to paronomasia, irony, chime, conceit, transitional similies, repudiation of the idea, antithesis and paradox.

Wheelwright has employed a more significant term, i.e., "plurisignation," to indicate the richness of meaning in poetry.[122] Ambiguity can be interpreted in more than one way in a sentence. Most ambiguities are, however, automatically

---

121 William Empson 19.

122 Philip Wheelwright, *The Burning Fountain* (Bloomington: Indiana UP, 1954), p. 101.

resolved by verbal context or by the situation in general in which communication takes place.

The phenomenon of multiple meanings, whether accidental or intentional, is not always a negative feature of language use. As Weinreich suggests, it is doubtful whether "an absolute distinction between true ambiguity and mere indefiniteness of reference can be maintained."[123] And it is this "indefiniteness of reference" that makes oblique poetry.

Linguistic and stylistic techniques have proved useful in the analysis of the verbal structure of poetry. As Culler points out:

> *... linguists [have] provided a number of concepts which could be used elleptically or metaphorically in discussing literary works... the use of such terms may help one to identify relations of various kinds, both actual and virtual, within a single level or between levels, which are responsible for the production of meaning.*[124]

The foremost among these concepts, Culler says, is the Saussurean dichotomy of langue and parole, which he regards as the basis of distinction on which modern linguistics rests. It would be worthwhile to consider the Indian theory of vakrokti in relation to Saussure's langue-parole distinction and Chomsky's treatment of "competence" and "performance."

The Indian thinking on poetry is largely centered around language. "*Vak*" has been accepted as the very base of the Indian thought. Poetry has been considered in India primarily in terms of linguistic organisation. The Sanskrit poetics gives due consideration to linguistic aspects while dealing with various elements of literary composition. A close examination

---

123 U. Weinreich, "Explorations in Semantic Theory," in *Current Trends in Linguistics. vol. III,* ed. T.A.Sebok (The Hague: Mouton, 1966), pp. 411-12.

124 Jonathan Culler, *Structuralist Poetics* (London: Routledge and Kegan Paul, 1975), p.8.

of the various aspects of Indian poetics will make it clear that Indian authorities on poetics never separated linguistics from poetics. While dealing with literary problems they also dealt with many intricate problems pertaining to linguistic behaviour. The Indian theory of stylistics made particular efforts to discover the general principles of poetic language.

The system built by Indian scholars is somewhat similar to that of generative grammar. It emphasizes at every point that the linguistic approach is the only approach which can help determine the patterns of beauty in literature.

Anandavardhana explored the nature of poetic meaning, and unfolded the function of words in poetic discourse. If classification, characterisation and meaning of relevant facts are accepted as the main objectives of science, then Anandavardhana's poetics must be said to have a scientific basis.

The linguistic orientation of Sanskrit poetics can be seen in alamkara and vastu dhvani. The basis of alamkara dhvani and vastu dhvani is essentially linguistic. Also, blemishes (dosas) are mostly classified on a linguistic basis. The general approach of Sanskrit poetics has been relatively objective in building a science of literature. S.K. De, however, takes this approch to be no better than that of textbooks and manuals. He attacks the Sanskrit poetics by saying that it ignores the poetic personality in the work of art and does not "satisfactorily explain as to why the work of one poet differs in character and quality from that of another poet, or why even two works of the same poet are not the same in these respects." He goes on to argue:

Sanskrit poetics purportedly engaged in solving the poetic riddle, delighted, rather in the pleasure of abstracted thought and formula calculation. Its method is suitable for the study of botany or zoology, but affords hardly any assistance for the understanding of aesthetic facts or principles. While it has an intuitive realization of the true nature of poetry, it allowed its intellectual prepossession to confine itself to the formulation of pedagogic expedients or normative abstractions. It is like studying the index of a book than the book itself.[125]

Though the Sanskrit critics were meticulously involved in "pedagogic expedients," as De argues, I would not completely agree with him that the Sanskrit critics were much concerned with "abstracted thought." What the Sanskrit critics have said about the nature of poetic langauge, the significance of suggestion as a semantic function, autonomy of literature, the nature of aesthetic perception, emotionality are all relevant for the modern scholars today. A comparative study would reveal that the Indian poetic tradition shares with the modern Western critical theories a central and practical interest in the way poetry should be analysed. It is only that Indian critics do not use Indian theories to analyse and evaluate modern literary text.

Kuntaka's and the Russian Formalists' approaches to the nature of poetic language have a striking similarity. Both were concerned with the basic problem of literariness in literature and strove to look into it in their own way by excluding non-literary agents. The point of departure between the two, however, is that Shlovsky, in the process of locating and understanding literariness of literature, demystified literature, in the process also de-mystifying the creator/writer. In the Indian scenario, this question did not arise because Indian writers never assumed any threat for literature and never felt the need to leave their biographical trace behind unlike the Westerners.

Kuntaka and the Formalists agreed on the fundamental principle of poetics lying in the distinction between poetic language and everyday language. This distinction could be seen in the opposition between *svabhavokti* (statement) and

---

125 S.K. De, *Sanskrit Poetics as a Study of Aesthetic* (Bombay: Oxford UP, 1963), pp. 78-79.

vakrokti (obliquity), between the language of familiarization and that of defamiliarization. *Svabhavokti* (scientific treatise) imparts knowledge and information, it removes ignorance but does not enhance perception, which is the work of poetic language. Similarly, Shklovsky believes that poetic language glorifies and enhances perception, whereas scientific language enhances recognition. However, Kuntaka's discussion of vakrokti and his views on language are more comprehensive than Shklovsky's concept of defamiliarization. Kuntaka's vakrokti anticipated the problem of literariness much before the Russian Formalist theory.

4

Russian Formalism and the Dialectics of Poetic Language

Viktor Shklovsky's 1914 essay on Futurist poetry, "The Ressurrection of the Word" marked the beginning of Russian Formalism. It was established as a full-fledged school of poetic theory but came to an end in 1930. The two groups of the Formalist school—the Opojaz group (The Society for the Study of Poetic Language) and the Moscow Linguistic Circle—were primarily interested in Russian Futurist poetry and in bringing poetic language into the field of linguistics. The Moscow Linguistic Circle had linguists like Roman Jakobson as members and the Petersburg-based Opojaz group, led by Viktor Shklovsky, had members like Boris Eikhenbaum, Osip Brik and Yury Tynyanov.

After the disintegration of the Formalist School in 1930 under intense political pressure, its ideas continued to survive in the Prague Linguistic Circle founded by Jakobson in 1926. The Prague Linguistic Circle included members like Rene Wellek, Jan Mukarovsky, N.S. Troubetzkoy and many others. Though the Formalist movement could not be established as a solid theoretical group, its influence on the Anglo-American critical movement in the 1950s and 60s has been enormous. Levi-Strauss's structural anthropology, the Parisian Structuralism in the 1960s, and especially the work of Todorov and Genette, looked back to Russian Formalism as a theoretical source.

The Russian Formalists, for the first time, tried to accord an independent position to literary studies. What they tried to do was to develop the very notion of the study of literature, or literary theory, not simply revising the previous schools of criticism. These critics changed the concept of genetic approach to literary studies. The genesis of a literary work had become the focus of most of the existing schools of criticism. So the study of literature had largely been a collective study of aesthetics, philosophy, psychology, history, sociology, etc. In such criticism, the study of literary aspects had become secondary and been relegated to the margins with the adjacent disciplines taking the centrestage. But all this changed when Formalists developed their theory of literary studies.

The study of literature in terms of biography, ethnography or history had made literature secondary to other disciplines. The Formalists did not even agree to the symbolists' definition of art as "thinking in images." For them this definition also reduced the scope of literary studies as an independent and specific discipline.

Both the Russian Formalism and the New Criticism are concerned with the effort to establish literary studies as an autonomous faculty. But Formalists were more inclined to a scientific approach than the New Critics who tend to move towards a humanistic understanding of a literary structure. The Formalists are opposed to the view that literature has a mimetic/ expressive function. They are more concerned with "literariness" than "literature." Literariness is what makes literature possible. So they were more interested to explore the system that makes literary discourse possible than literature itself.

The Formalist theory of literary study was even more radical and systematic than that of the New Critics. While the New Critics speculated and explored the relation between literature and life, art and value, the Formalists saw literature and life, art and value as opposites. Some New Critics like I.A.

Richards were also concerned with making literary studies scientific with the help of physiology, or neuro-psychology, which the Formalists considered non-literary. Unlike the narrow textual approach of the New Critics, the Russian Formalists were innovative and anticipated the developments of literary studies in the 1960s which were based on modern linguistics.

The Russian Formalists aimed at establishing literary studies as an autonomous genre. As Eikhenbaum remarks, Formalism is "neither an aesthetic nor a methodology" but is "characterised only by the attempt to create an independent science of literature which studies specifically literary material." So for the Formalists "the question is not how to study literature, but what the subject matter of literary study actually is ?"[126]

The Formalists work on the concept of "differential specification," their definition of literature being different from the sets of other things. The study of literary science is to examine the set of differences that distinguish literature from other objects. This differential set is known as "defamiliarization" or "making strange" (*ostranenie*). The term "*priem ostranenie*" ("device of making strange" or alienation/estrangement) which has its origin in Aristotle, has undergone a process of development through its use in the neoclassical "baroque" poetics, German romantic literary theory and finally in the Russian Formalism in its new incarnation. Defamiliarization is a device which makes strange the habitual perception in ordinary language. Shklovsky says that when every object of the world becomes familiar to us, we become habituated to that object. Our everyday life then becomes a life of "prose perceptions," which means, things become

126 Boris Eikhenbaum, "The Theory of the Formal Method," in *Russian Formalism*, ed. and trans. Lee T. Lemon and Marion J. Reis (Lincoln: University of Nebraska Press, 1965), pp. 102-103.

known but not perceived. The process of perceiving this world becomes so automatic that the objects no longer register upon our senses. "Habitualization devours works, clothes, furniture, one's wife, and the fear of war." Against this prose perception, there is the world of art which, Shklovsky says, "exists that one may recover the sensation of life; it exists to make one feel things, to make the stone *stony*. The purpose of art is to impart the sensation of things as they are perceived and not as they are known."[127]

The end or purpose of art is not what Shklovsky suggests here to experience the "artfulness of an object"; he is more interested with the way art accomplishes this purpose. This technique is a process which transforms perception into a transcendent activity. In this process of defamiliarization, the worldly object is taken out of the area of prose perception and placed in the arena of art. The technique of art is to make objects '*unfamiliar*,' to make forms difficult, to increase the difficulty and length of perception, because the process of perception is an aesthetic end in itself and must be prolonged. As Shklovsky says, "*Art is a way of experiencing the artfulness of an object; the object is not important*."[128] (Shklovsky's emphasis). It draws our attention to the artifice of the literary text. Art, according to Shklovsky, defamiliarizes the usual or habitual things. For instance, walking is an ordinary and habitual activity, which is defamiliarized in dancing. The usual, everyday activity of walking is refreshed and perceived anew in dancing. According to Shklovsky, "A dance is a walk which is felt even more accurately, it is a walk which is constructed to be felt."[129]

127 Viktor Shklovsky, "Art as Technique," in *Russian Formalism*, ed. and trans. Lee T. Lemon and Marion J. Reis (Lincoln: University of Nebraska Press, 1965), p.19.

128 Viktor Shklovsky "Art as Technique,"p. 19.

129 Viktor Shklovsky, "On the connection between the devices of syuzhet construction and general stylistic devices," in *Russian Formalism: A Collection of Articles and Texts in Translation*," ed. Stephen Bann and John E. Bowlt (New York: Barnes, 1973), p. 48.

So also is poetry different from ordinary language, because ordinary/practical language is made strange by art. The language of poetry is "oblique," "torturous," "difficult" and "attenuated." The physical sound of words used in everyday language, when defamiliarized, becomes prominent; this formal prominence is the basis of poetry. This is what Shklovsky says, "Poetic speech is *formed* speech, because defamiliarization is found almost everywhere form is found."[130]

The Russian Formalists focused primarily on the analysis of poetic language on the basis of the difference between the poetic and everyday language. What distinguishes literature from practical language is its constructed quality. Poetry exercises a controlled violence upon practical language, which is thereby deformed and compels our attention to its constructed nature. For them, literary studies consist of the study of especially the poetic language, as themes are inconsistent and tend to be centrifugal. Poetry is highlighted only when it is studied in the context of what is not poetry. The notion of literariness, which is central to the Formalist school, is achieved by the process of differentiation. It also gives literary studies a scientific status, which helps in understanding the coherence of the system.

The poetic language is different from the practical/communicative language. The language of poetry and the practical language have very different functions. The practical language is used for communicative purpose, whereas the language of poetry has no such practicality. The Formalists' sharp differentiation between the poetic and the practical use of language has helped in evolving a scientific basis for the study of literature. Jakobson sees the difference between the poetic and practical language in terms of their autotelic and heterotelic natures, respectively.

The poetic language effects a two-fold shift of perception, as Tony Bennett rightly says, "Literature offers not only

---

130 Viktor Shklovsky, "Art as Technique", p. 18.

a new insight into 'reality,' but also reveals the formal operations whereby what is commonly taken for 'reality', is constructed."[131] The poetic language is distinguished from the ordinary language not because of the difference in structure or vocabulary, but because the use of the formal devices like rhythm and rhyme transforms the ordinary into something special. The technique of defamiliarization acts upon and is realized by the formal devices. But the term "formalist" is a misnomer, as Eikhenbaum said, because it was used as a pejorative term by its opponents. According to Eikhenbaum, "They were not 'formalists', but, if you like–'specifiers'."[132] For, "the formalists' preoccupation with form derived from their preoccupation with the specificity of literariness and never constituted an end in itself."[133]

In subsequent developments of Formalism, the opposition between the habitual and defamiliarization was seen as no longer located outside literature. It was no longer a differentiation between ordinary language and poetic language, but one located within literature itself. For Shklovsky, form itself is the defamiliarizing element which can also prove to be an automatizing factor at times. He says, "There is 'order' in art, yet not a single column of a Greek temple stands exactly in its proper order; poetic rhythm is similarly disordered rhythm... should the disordering of rhythm become a convention, it would be ineffective as a device for the roughening of language."[134]

The literary devices, which are meant to defamiliarize automatized perception, do not succeed in doing so. They need to be constantly renovated to produce conditions for defamiliarization. For the Formalists, the literary tradition is not

131 Tony Bennett, *Formalism and Marxism* (London: Methuen, 1979), p.54

132 L. M. O' Tool and Ann Shukman, "A Contextual Glossary of Formalist Terminology," *Russian Poetics in Translation* 4 (1977), p. 20.

133 Ann Jefferson and David Robey, eds. *Modern Literary Theory* (London: B.T. Batsford Ltd., 1986), p. 29.

134 Viktor Shklovsky, 24.

a seamless continuity but rather a discontinuity giving scope for the constant regeneration of formal devices for the renewal of the system. The concept of "literariness" gives a systematic inflection to the study of literature, going beyond the intrinsic study of the individual text.

Shklovsky believed that the new literary production always deliberately deviates from the poetic norms of the preceding literary movement. Jakobson's and Tynyanov's notion of the "dominant" is similar to Shklovsky's concept of defamiliarization; it allows the "foregrounding" of the dominant device in the literary text pushing the other devices to the background. The same happens in case of literary evolution; the prevailing canonical forms and genres are replaced by new forms, which in turn would become canonized and, likewise, be replaced by still newer forms. Some elements in a literary work have a defamiliarizing effect, and these elements are foregrounded against the group of elements which are in the background. "Since a system is not a free interplay of equal elements," Tynyanov comments, "but presupposes the foregrounding of one group of elements ('a dominant') and the deformation of others, a work becomes literature and acquires its literary function through just this dominance."[135]

The distinction between "device" and "function" becomes prominent in the Formalist rhetoric while considering literature as a system with a coherence and unity, and where the function of the devices is decided between defamiliarization or automatization. Since differentiation is no longer seen outside literature, there exists a more tolerant and flexible relationship between the literary and non-literary, helping the Formalists to maintain the "literary" nature in their enquiry. Literary studies, for the Formalists, remains a science with "literariness" as its object, which is achieved by the technique of differentia between defamiliarization and automatization.

135 L.M.O' Toole and Ann Shukman, 34.

The two related concepts, the principle of perceptible form and the idea of the structural significance of literary content, developed by the Russian Formalists, are first taken into consideration by Viktor Shklovsky. Shklovsky's argument depends upon the distinction between "automatized" and aesthetic forms of perception. He says, "If we start to examine the general laws of perception, we see that as perception becomes habitual it becomes automatic."[136]

Literature transforms our habitual mode of perception in two ways. According to Tony Bennett, "First, particularly with regard to poetry, literature was said to effect a semantic shift in relation to prosaic language by playing on and subverting the conventional relationship between signifier and signified, opening up the web of language into a play of multiple meanings excluded from ordinary speech. Second, literary works were said to defamiliarize the codes and conventions of previous traditions which, although they had once themselves served as a means of perpetual dislocation, have since atrophied to become the source of perpetual numbness."[137]

The object exists as an image of the real world but, unlike the supporters of mimetic theory, Shklovsky believes that the meaning of the image should be seen in its relation to the work as a whole, where it functions as a structural device, a technique of formation, and not as a representation of the world of experience. So he writes, "Poets are much more concerned with arranging images than with creating them,"[138] because it is not the content of images but the way they are placed and organised in the whole network of relationships that is important. As Shklovsky writes, "The meaning of a work broadens to the extent that artfulness and artistry diminish."[139] Based on the

136 Viktor Shklovsky, 11.

137 Tony Bennett, 55.

138 Viktor Shklovsky, 7.

139 Viktor Shklovsky, 19-20.

opposition of form and meaning, Shklovsky defines his concept of poetic language. To him, meaning is the function of prose utterence, it is the process of abstracting the essences of words rather than their sensible form. The poetic utterance is opposed to this. "The language of poetry," Shklovsky observes," "is... difficult, roughened, impeded language....We can define poetry as *attenuated, torturous* speech. Poetic speech is *formed speech.* Prose is ordinary speech–economical, easy, proper... of the accurate, facile type, of the 'direct' expression of the child."[140]

For Shklovsky, defamiliarization is found almost in every form of art. He goes on to say:

> *An image is not a permanent referent for those mutable complexities of life which are revealed through it; its purpose is not to make us perceive meaning, but to create a special perception of the object–it creates a 'vision' of the object instead of serving as a means for knowing it.*[141]

He does not consider any literary text as an end in itself, to be read for its own sake and on its own terms; rather he thinks that a literary text is sought as a mode for justifying or verifying the exemplification and development of the concept of literariness.

The Formalists' claim that the purpose of literary criticism is not to view literary text as something "already there" or "pre-given," but to study what makes literature different from non-literature. Tony Bennett argues for the Formalists:

> *This difference consisted in the tendency of literary works to defamiliarize experience by working on and transforming the adjacent ideological and cultural forms within which reality is dominantly experienced. The prime task for literary criticism became that of analysing the constructional devices whereby this effect of defamiliarization was achieved. The object of the Formalists' research was thus not the concrete object of literary*

140 Viktor Shklovsky, 22-23.

141 Viktor Shklovsky, 21.

texts themselves but the abstract object of the differential relation between literary texts and non-literary texts, a problematic (in the sense defined above) that was entirely the product of their own theoretical procedures.[142]

Literariness achieved through the technique of defamiliarization is not limited to the intrinsically formal properties of the text alone; it has an inherently relational basis with factors working outside the domain of literature. To view a text as literary, the context of the non-literary has to be brought in.

The literary devices defamiliarization depends on are not merely formal devices used to decorate a text. The effect of "literariness" depends instead on the function of these literary devices in the text, the devices used in some texts help in bringing wonderful effects of making strange the conventional themes whereas in others they are not equally effective. In some cases, the same device has different functions in different texts. The function of the devices not only determines the effectiveness of texts in their efforts to defamiliarize the conventions, it also helps in distinguishing the literary from the non-literary. For example, the poetic language is distinguished from the prosaic language not because the former uses poetic devices like metaphors but because both use metaphors for different purposes. Elrich remarks:

If in informative prose, a metaphor aims to bring the subject closer to the audience or drive a point home in 'poetry,' it serves as a means of intensifying the intended aesthetic effect. Rather than translating the unfamiliar into the terms of the familiar, the poetic image 'makes strange' the habitual by presenting it in a novel light, by placing it in an unexpected context.[143]

---

142 Tony Bennett, 44-50.

143 Viktor Erlich Qtd. Tony Bennett, 51.

Shklovsky's distinction between the ordinary and the poetic language is reformulated by the Prague Structuralists, especially by Bohuslav Havranek and Jan Mukarovsky. For the Prague Structuralists, the distinction exists between the utterances whose language is automatized and those where it is foregrounded. In foregrounding, language is deautomatized, like a poetic metaphor.

The concept of foregrounding pushes linguistics to the brink of poetics. Mukarovsky observes, "In poetic language foregrounding achieves maximum intensity to the extent of pushing communication into the background as the objective of expression and of being used for its own sake; it is not used in the services of communication but in order to place in the foreground the act of expression, the act of speech itself."[144]

Though literariness is the distinctive feature of literature, the Formalists accept the position where literariness co-exists with other elements. But by redefining the literary work as a "hierarchical set of artistic devices," rather than a "sum total of all devices," they very cleverly have brought in the concept of the dominant where the co-existence of the elements was seen as one being subordinated by the other. It is always the literery factor that dominates other factors in a text. Roman Jakobson defines the "dominant" as "the focusing component of a work of art which rules, determines and transforms the remaining components."[145] To illustrate his definition, he points to three different periods of the Czech poetic tradition where the three devices—rhyme, syllabic scheme and intonational integrity—are present but each becomes dominant at different points of time, a fact which, he believes, is always historically determined

---

144 Jan Mukarovsky, "Standard Language and Poetic Language," in *A Prague School Reader on Esthetics, Literary Structure, and Style*, ed. and trans. Paul L. Garvin (Washington D.C.: Georgetown UP, 1964), p. 19.

145 Roman Jakobson, "The Dominant," in *Readings in Russian Poetics: Formalist and Structural Views*, ed. Ladishav Matejka and Krystyna Pomorska (Cambridge, Mass.: MIT Press, 1971), p. 82.

and depends on the concept of the "dominant." This definition includes both a historical approach and a linguistic analysis, moving beyond the synchronic/diachronic distinction.

The concept of the dominant helps in viewing literature in more distinctive terms. This could be seen in the distinction between the literary and non-literary, in the difference between the Renaissance modes of seeing and the Romantic modes of hearing or in the differences in the various literary genres in the same era or in the differentiating qualities of the works of contemporary writers.

In this sense, Jakobson's definition of the poetic work as "a verbal message, whose aesthetic function is dominant,"[146] includes a host of other functions as well. Here pure formalism gives way to a historical approach where literariness is definitely sought but the other function of defamiliarization is seen in a historically conditioned environment. Jakobson thus remarks,

> *The reader of a poem or the viewer of a painting has a vivid awareness of two orders: the traditional canon and the artistic novelty as a deviation from the canon. It is precisely against the background of that tradition that innovation is conceived. The formalist studies brought to light that this simultaneous preservation of tradition and breaking away from tradition form the essence of every new work of art.*[147]

The Formalists also anticipate the futurist concept of the "trans-sense language," i.e., language containing in itself a sense of its unintelligibility. Shklovsky's categorization of folklores, nursery-rhymes, religious rituals in the group of trans-sense language is based on his argument that in these kinds of work sound is more important than sense. From this he infers that in the language used in poetry sound has a more

---

146 Roman Jakobson, 84.

147 Roman Jakobson, 85.

prominent place than sense. By proclaiming the supremacy of sound over sense he makes a deliberate break with the earlier school of symbolists, who took every sound/word of the poem as having a symbolic function.

Paul Valery, too, believes that the intelligibility of poetic act is not semantic but formal. In poetry, Valery writes, "language is no longer a transitive act, an expedient. On the contrary, it has its own value, which must remain intact in spite of the operations of the intellect on the given propositions. Poetic language must preserve itself, through itself, and remain the same, not to be altered by the act of intelligence that finds or gives it a meaning."[148] For Valery, the opposition between form and meaning is a way of describing the peculiar dynamism of poetic speech. He gives the example of an oscillating pendulum:

> *Think of a pendulum oscillating between two symmetrical points. Suppose that one of these extremes represents form: the concrete characteristics of language, sound, rhythm, accent, tone, movement–in a word, the Voice in action. Then associate with the other point, ... all significant values, images and ideas, stimuli of feeling and memory, virtual impulses and structures of understanding in short, everything that makes the content, the meaning of the discourse. Now observe the effect of poetry on yourselves. You will find that at each line the meaning produced within you, far from destroying the musical form communicated to you, recalls it. The living pendulum that has swung from sound to sense swings back to its felt point of departure, as though the very sense which is present to your mind can find no other outlet or expression, no other answer, than the very music which gave it birth.*[149]

148 Paul Valery, *The Art of Poetry* (London: Routledge, 1958), pp. 170-171.

149 Paul Valery, 72.

This example implies that though the opposition between meaning and form continues, there is an attempt to harmonize them. In poetry thus the semantic components take on structural value.

Valery's concept of poetic language is different from that of the New Critics'. The New Critics argue for poetry as a form of signification which is superior to science. But for Valery, however, poetry is a form of signification only to the extent that "the thoughts uttered or suggested by the text of a poem are by no means the unique and cheif objects of its discourse—but means which combine equally with the sounds, cadences, meter, and ornaments to produce and sustain a particular tension or exaltation, to engender within us a world, or mode of existence, of complete harmony."[150]

In poetry, Valery believes, sounds display meaning not as idea but simply as sounds because language tends to be self-revealing rather than being a mere medium. The sounds of words modify the act of speech in such a way that this activity itself becomes an integral part of the meaning of the work. Valery remarks: "It is an error contrary to the nature of poetry, and one which may even be fatal to it, to claim that for each poem there is a corresponding true meaning, unique and comfortable to, or identical with, some thought of the author's."[151] In poetry, there is no "true meaning; meaning is characterized by the condition of indeterminancy."[152]

However, Mukarovsky attacks the view that in poetry the maximum foregrounding is achieved by foregrounding each and every component in it. For him, foregrounding is an activity which is selective and systematic because what

150 Paul Valery, 147.

151 Paul Valery, 27.

152 E.D. Hirsch, *Validity in Interpretation* (New Haven: Yale UP 1967), pp. 44-46.

is foregrounded in poetic utterance is a complex of multiple inter-relationships among linguistic components. He remarks:

> *There is always present, in communicative speech... the potential relationship between intonation and meaning, syntax, word order, or the relationship of the word as a meaningful unit to the phonetic structure of the text, to the lexical selection found in the text, to other words as units of meaning in the context of the same sentence. It can be said that each linguistic component is linked directly or indirectly, by means of these multiple inter-relationships, in some way to every other component. In communicative speech these relationships are for the most part merely potential, because attention is not called to their presence and to their mutual relationship.*[153]

In ordinary speech, the manifold relationships among the linguistic components are present largely as a structural possibility, but in poetic speech this possibility is actualized when these manifold relationships are brought to the foreground.

The Formalists choose to call their method morphological so as to differentiate it from other methods like the sociological, historical and to suggest that content is determined by form. Form was considered so important that content was relegated to background and was seen as something dependent on form in a work's aesthetic structure. Shklovsky in his pamphlet "The Ressurection of the Word" gave an independent position to form and wrote that the "artistic perception is perception in which form is sensed perhaps not only form, but form as an essential part."[154] Five years later, he writes in a revisionist mode, "A new form appears not in order to express a new

153 Jan Mukarovsky, 20-21.

154 Viktor Shklovsky, "The Ressurection of the Word." in *Russian Formalism : A Collection of Articles and Texts in Translation*, ed. Stephen Bann and John E. Bowlt (New York: Barnes, 1973), p. 41-42.

content, but in order to replace an old form, which has already lost its artistic value." [155] The distinction of form and content was, however, necessary for the Formalists because of their complete opposition to realism in any form. For form to be possible and effective, it is important to make use of special artistic devices such as *defamiliarization* and *retardation*.

By nature, defamiliarization seems opposed to the principle of artistic economy which implies that the unfamiliar is explained in terms of the familiar poetic images. In defamiliarization the opposite takes place: the familiar is described in unfamiliar terms. The worldly things are made strange and this principle is the central objective of avant-garde art. Here life and nature are not described in neat packages of predictable images, but the relationship between them is distorted, disrupted and divided through certain unusual poetic devices.

A part of the process of the defamilarization involves the special use of rhythm. Rhythm, the dominant element in poetry, is not just added for poetic euphony; it has a dynamic function. The Formalists never confused rhythm with meter. Rhythm deforms the meaning of a poem and, as Erlich says, "brings words closer to each other, makes them interact, overlap, crisscross, and in so doing, reveals the wealth of this 'lateral' potential meaning." Quoting Eikhenbaum, he goes on to say, "The play of these lateral meanings running afoul as it does of habitual verbal associations, is the principal feature of poetic semantics."[156]

The Formalists approach prosody in a different way. According to them, prosody must not be a study in phonetics, but should aim at phonemics, which is the study of the linguistic functions of speech sounds and their capacity for differentiating word-meaning. They opposed the sound-meaning dichotomy.

---

155 Viktor Shklovsky, 23.

156 Viktor Erlich, *Russian Formalism: History-Doctrine,* 3rd ed. (New Haven: Yale UP, 1981), p. 225.

The two sets of references, namely, "poetic euphony" and "poetic imagery" are intrinsic to the verse which is a self-contained entity.

Retardation, another device like defamiliarization, means the slowing down of action. The aesthetic process of perception needs to be prolonged for greater enjoyment of art. According to Shklovsky, the readers can sustain their interest in art by reading beyond the "wall of strangeness" built around the art form. The concept of retardation is also found in Anandavardhana's *Dhvanyaloka* where the author suggests that a *sahradaya* (connossieur) is one who goes beyond the literal to have a full grasp of a literary work in a slow process of cognition. Anandavardhana says this in the context of semantics. While speaking of the factors leading to suggestion, the Formalists have emphasized the formal devices and techniques.

The Formalists are also interested in what was called the "inventive" (*izobretatelstvo*), which means "bold innovation," and various ways of "toying with the narrative." Gogol, Cervantes, Sterne fascinated the Formalists because of their use of this technique. Tolstoy also impressed Shklovsky for his ironic treatment of events, irony in the Greek sense "eiron" which means, one who affects ignorance.

Shklovsky brings in the term "defacilitation" (*Zatrulnenie*) while criticizing the *positivist* thought which believed in the "law of conservation of energy" where the writer does not exert much effort to express an idea or a theme. He, on the other hand, gives ample examples from Russian folk literature to illustrate how defacilitation is used for purely aesthetic purposes, to deliberately make the subject difficult or to impede the idea by using difficult words or syntax, turning the conventional mode of narrative or metre upside down. In Erlich's term, "It is verbal tight-rope walking," or as he quotes Shklovsky, it is "a unique kind of dancing of the speech organs."[157]

157 Viktor Erlich, 178.

The concept of "laying bare the device" (*obnazhenie priema*) is a technique writers use to "lay bare" a literary convention within a literary text. The glaring example is Sterne's *Tristram Shandy* where Sterne has a chapter dealing with chapters revealing his stylistic device. Grossvogel remarks, "Structural subtlties that would normally be hidden within the fictional weave of the novel, Sterne deliberately exposes for the purpose of turning his book into yet another kind of parlor game which he plays with his reader."[158] This device emphasizes what the Formalists would like to say about the content becoming the form.

While discussing the prose narrative, the Formalists apply two terms—*fabula* and *syuzhet*. The first refers to the "story" or the "raw material"; the second refers to "plot" or the "aesthetically ordered presentation" of the story. As the poetic language is distinguished from the ordinary language, so also is the story distinguished from the plot in a literary prose narrative. For Shklovsky, the creativity in a literary piece is discernible in *syuzhet (plot)*, the way in which a story is constructed. "Story is," defines Tomashevsky, "the sum total of events, mutually and internally linked, (i.e. the total number of motifs, linked causally and temporarily together)," whereas plot is the distribution and construction of events in order; the plot is the literary examination of the motifs, "an artistically constructed distribution of events."[159] The story is a "stock" or "pre-aesthetic" material from which the plot is constructed.

The connection of Flaubert's desire to write a purely formal novel with the Formalist doctrine has some interesting aspects. Flaubert, in one of his letters, writes,

---

158 D. Grossvogel, *Limits of the Novel* (Ithaca: Cornell UP, 1971), p. 148.

159 . Richard Sherwood, "Viktor Shklovsky and the Development of Early Formalist Theory on Prose literature," in *Russian Formalism*, ed. Stephen Bann and John E. Bowlt (New York: Barnes, 1973), p. 33.

What strikes me as beautiful, what I should like to do, is a book about nothing, a book without external attachments, which would hold together by itself through the internal force of its style... a book which would have practically no subject, or at least one in which the subject would be almost invisible, if that is possible.[160]

The device of tautological repetition leads to retardation where the action does not stop but slows down. If the story material is "a" then a literary work is expressed by the formula: a + (a+a) + [a+(a+a)] + ... etc. For Shklovsky, "the heart of literary device" consists in this formula. It is not just the story element *a* but the formula, as Richard Sherwood says, with all its "elaborations, complications, repetitions of the story so constructed that the work is truly 'perceived,' the process of perception being heightened by 'retardation' which serves to extend and intensify the perceptive process."[161] Shklovsky's notion of the "evolutionary ability of art" is connected with this device of tautological repetition. What Shklovsky means by the evolutionary ability of art is that each new school which evolves is first parodied and then gives way to another new school. It is only by a constant process of change and contrast that the artistic qualities of each school / art are evident.

The role of the writer as an organiser of materials, "taking one piece and putting it beside the other pieces" and applying selected devices is an important aspect in creative process. In his introduction to his collected essays on prose literature, Shklovsky says, "In the theory of literature I am concerned with analysing its internal law. To an analogy in industrial terms, I am interested not in the situation of the world cotton market, not in the politics of the cotton combines, but only

---

160 Flaubert Qtd. G. Becker, ed. *Documents in Modern Literary Realism* (Princeton: Princeton UP, 1967), p. 90.

161 Richard Sherwood, 36.

in the numbers of the thread and the ways of weaving it."[162] This analogy is significant as it implies that a work of art is constituted by linked metaphors enriching each other in a process of complex relationship. Roman Jakobson's insistence that not literature but literariness should be the actual field of inquiry of literary science stands justified. What Jakobson is trying to say is that it is not the text/literary work itself which is to be analyzed, it is rather the devices employed in the text which help the literary analyst in his examination.

The Formalists believe that poetics is not the study of "chaotic images" in their inchoate relationships, but is concerned with a conceptual system which can identify devices working in an individual work. So, poetics is concerned with the system of discourse, which is the generative principle of every text.

Shklovsky's early essays like "The Resurrection of the Word" and "Art as Device" addressed some essential Formalist ideas adopted from the previous theories. Here while attacking Aleksandre Potebnya and Aleksandre Veselovsky for their theories, he has also borrowed many ideas from them which he could utilize in his theorization. Potebnya's interpretation of the gradual loss of form in the "journey from poetry to prose" is the starting point for the Formalists to distinguish between the language of poetry and ordinary language. Potebnya's conception that the "internal form"(image) is different from the "external form" (sound) and that the "internal form" (image) is the hallmark of poetic language which decides the external form (sound) is reversed in the Formalist thinking. Shklovesky claims that "external form" (sound) is the actual hallmark of poetic language.

For Potebnya, the difference between poetic and prosaic language was in their *means*, not in their *purpose*. For the Formalists, the difference is in the purpose. Content, so important for Potebnya, was dismissed by the Formalists,

162 Viktor Shklovsky, 118.

who replaced form and content with the form and material. Shklovsky went to the extent of saying that the form "creates its own content." Whereas Potebnya emphasized the psychological impact of the author on his writing, Shklovsky speaks of the effect of the text on the reader, focusing on the process of "sensing" the text.

Another aspect of Shklovsky's theory is that it did not accept Veselovsky's theory of the social role of "epithet in language." On the other hand, he never believed that epithet was a result of the intrinsic evolution in language, which is similar to the Indian concept of rasa and rasa-realization. In response to his own question as to why Ovid recommends *unhurried enjoyment* by creating "Art of Love," he replies that the nature of art itself is like a "crooked road" which turns back on itself.

Another area which gives Shklovsky's theory a distinctive flavour is his difference between *"motif"* (motif) and *"plot"* (syuzhet) in studying prose literature. He defines *motif* as the "simplest narrative unit," while plot is the composition of different motifs. He seems to think that while motif is an essential requirement for the plot, it should not always be linked with real life. Potebnya's and Veselovsky's keen sense of history and of the effect of time on language had a tremendous impact on their theory of language and literature. Shklovsky does not agree to this view.

However, he does not completely reject the relation of motif to real life; he admits that real-life experiences influence, thereby partially admitting the influence of life on art. He accepts history and society as the sources of art, but he thinks that what an art critic or a student of literary studies should do is to identify the artistic quality of art without involving oneself in the extraneous factors which historians, ethnographers or anthropologists are concerned with. To him, literature is not directly influenced by life but can be seen as an index of formal changes taking place in different kinds of literature as a result of changes in society.

In differentiating the poetic from the prosaic language, Shklovsky interprets the two not as genres of poetry and prose but as two systems of language having two specific functions. The poetic language includes not only the genre of poetry but all forms of literature including prose which are structured for artistic impression; prosaic language is the language used for ordinary communication. So the Formalists account for the differences in genre by the different sets of devices used. Shklovsky mentions that poetry has better "geometricality of the devices" than prose.

The traditional rhetoricians saw figurative speech as a kind of "abuse" or "trespassing" of common utterances or as a turning from common modes of writing and speaking and did not distinguish keenly between ordinary and poetic speech but tried to give "laws" or "formula" of style by which ordinary speech could be transformed. Henry Peacham and George Puttenham viewed ordinary language as an ideal combination of word and thing and literary language a distance between the two where the word instead of pointing to a referential world creates its own verbal world.

But Russian Formalists conceived form as the result of the combination of what they call deformation and organisation. Deformation is a process through which changes are brought about in ordinary language so that they acquire poetic character through defamiliarization. Form is used here in a broader sense that includes also the content. In this sense the distinction between the two–form and content–is abolished. Later they used a more comprehensive term "structure" instead of form to avoid the limited implication of the word "form."

The Formalists criticized the symbolists' overemphasis on visual imagination. They were also not very comfortable with the Marxist view of the importance of history. They were deliberately anti-historical. Instead, they tried to study the evolution of the different artistic devices which goes through a process of deautomatization and ultimately becomes automatized giving way to newer devices.

They, however, did not completely deny the social function of art. On the contrary, they redefined and broadened its scope by asserting that art makes us see things which we usually tend to ignore. In this way art is related to life.

Jan Mukarovsky developed the concept of defamiliarisation more systematically than Shklovsky by trying to include the extra-literary factors. He says that art leads to a "renewed awareness of the manifold and multivalent nature of reality."[163] Art helps us focus our attention on signs themselves instead of taking them for granted by subverting the conventional sign systems. The Prague school viewed the structure of the individual text as a system of signs. Mukarovsky remarks:

> *The mutual relationship of the components of the work of poetry, both foregrounded and unforegrounded, constitute its structure, a dynamic structure including both convergence and divergence, and one that constitutes an indissociable artistic whole, since each of its components has its value in terms of its relation to the totality.*[164]

So the aim of literary studies is to identify deviations from existing linguistic and literary practice. This involves the analysis of the language as well as the content of the text. The concept of the "dominant" provides an important element for analysis of text. As Mukarovsky says, all components of the text and their interrelationships "are evaluated from the standpoint of the dominant," which thus "creates the unity of the work of poetry."[165]

163 Paul L. Garvin, ed. and trans. *A Prague School Reader on Esthetics, Literary Structure, and Style* (Washington D.C.: Georgetown UP, 1964), p. 33.

164 Garvin 22.

165 Garvin 20-21.

Mukarovsky's notion of the "aesthetic structure" does not, however, exclude extra-literary factors from critical analysis. He emphasized the dynamic tension between literature and society in a literary text and agreed that the aesthetic function proves to be an ever shifting boundary and not a category. The sphere of art is always changing and is dynamically related to the structure of society. Art and literature are thus constantly being defined as the literary canon is deconstructed.

Mukarovsky seems to be influenced by Yury Tynyanov. Yury Tynyanov made two new and significant contributions. According to R.H. Stacy, "The first involves his concept of the dynamic rather than static nature of literary phenomena, i.e., the ever-changing nature of literature, the fluidity of the boundary between literature and life and a rejection of *a priori* definitions (to pay more attention to the importance of the historical and sociological background in the study of literature). For Tynyanov, literature is, 'dynamic verbal structure.' He looked upon literature as a 'system of system' rather than, in Shklovskian terms, a 'sum total of literary device.' He argues for the study of art as dynamic integration, as aesthetic structure, and not as the mere enumeration of coexisting elements, one of the less satisfying aspects of Shklovsky's method."[166]

Mikhail Bakhtin, however, criticized the Formalists for neglecting social and ideological concerns in poetic language. The Marxists and other emerging literary groups like the Bakhtin Linguistic Circle attacked the Formalists because they failed to provide an adequate sociological and philosophical justification for their theories. In their search for literariness they excluded all that was non-literary. But the distinction of literary and non-literary is problematic. I think Roger Webster is right when he says that "it is dangerous to have rigid categories and

---

166 R. H. Stacy, *Russian Literary Criticism: A Short History* (Syrause: Syrause UP, 1974), p. 175.

boundaries as to literary and non-literary discourse. Literary discourse is a relative category both formally and historically and thus liable to change and open to redefinition. Its formal characteristics emerge by differentiation from other kinds of language, and its historical nature by differentiation from–or compliance with–official and conventional discourses."[167]

Many critics view that Bakhtin's work is not very distinct in approach from the Formalists. Bakhtin's work is historically connected to the aims of the Formalist movement. Though Bakhtin is concerned with novel and Jakobson with poetry, one would agree with Ann Jefferson that "Bakhtin and Jakobson share the same underlying assumptions: first that literature is instructive about the nature of language; and secondly, that the function of literature... is to focus attention on the message."[168] So literature is a self-referential use of language and language has multiple components. Bakthin attributes these assumptions to the social and Jakobson to the structural.

Despite the attempt of Jakobson, Tynyanov and Mukarovsky to connect the aims of Formalism to larger social and cultural issues, Formalism remained committed to the notion that "literariness" alone was the aim of literary studies.

---

167 Roger Webster, *Studying Literary Theory* (London: Arnold, 1990), p. 46.

168 Ann Jefferson, "Literariness, Dominance and Violence in Formalist Aesthetics," in *Literary Theory Today* ed. Peter Collier and Helga Geyer Ryan (Ithaca: Cornell UP, 1990), p. 138.

5

The Aesthetics of Form and New Criticism

The New Criticism as a literary theory and criticism began roughly with the works of I. A. Richards and T. S. Eliot and was developed and continued by American critics like John Crowe Ransom, W. K. Wimsatt, Cleanth Brooks and Allen Tate from the 1940s to the 1960s. The affinities of the New Criticism with Russian Formalism and the Prague School are really striking and surprisingly so despite the fact that the New Critics apparently knew nothing of the Formalist school. This is evident from Wimsatt and Brooks's *Literary Criticism: A Short History* (1957) which makes no reference to this school.

The New Critical theories are similar to the tenets of the Formalist thought in their association that a literary work is distinct from a non-literary text and is defined in terms of these distinctions. Both significantly emphasised the importance of structure in a literary work and organic relationships between the various components of a text and between the parts to the whole. Both look upon a text as independent of its author and socio-historical context.

The New Criticism, despite its many conceptual drawbacks and orthodox ideology, still continues to be a major contribution to literary theory, Anglo-American community, particularly among men who are in the teaching profession in the universities and colleges. Though their assumptions about literature and literary study seem somewhat irrelevant in the context of contemporary theories, their influence in the academics cannot be ignored. These assumptions are still considered as an alternative for those who like to see literature more concerned with life than with a rigid formalistic structure. The New Critics believed that literature is related with reality/"real" world in many ways and helps one coping with life, whereas Formalism was least interested in connecting literature with the world outside. In this sense, the New Critical approach was empiricist and humanistic.

I. A. Richards', *The Principles of Literary Criticism*, published in 1924, *The Meaning of Meaning* (written collectively with C.K. Ogden) and *Practical Criticism* exercised a dominant influence on the New Criticism and consequently on the way literature was taught in British and American universities for five decades. He had an enormous impact on literary theory, criticism, teaching of literature and university curriculum.

Richards' theories are important for several reasons. They tried to explain the significance of poetry in terms of the meanings of words. Richards' analytical thoroughness and comprehensiveness resulted from his experiments in the classroom. Words, according to Richards, have no fixed meaning; their sense is enriched by "neighbour words" and also by the contexts in which they have previously occurred. This is the full implication of what he calls the "interinanimation" of words. The significance of a word, he implies, can be gathered by what is called "an attitude of alert irrelevance."

He also suggests that the significance of a sentence is not realized by adding together the fixed meanings of words; rather words get their value from their togetherness and enter into infinitely subtler and more manifold relations among themselves. A sentence, to him "being the act of an organism, is itself an organism." Ambiguity, thus, is not a stylistic fault but an inevitable consequence of the powers of language and an indispensable means of poetic utterance. The poetic experience is more highly and delicately organized than ordinary experience.

William Empson, Richards' student, chose to highlight one aspect of poetry that is definable in terms of the medium. The poetic language is differentiated from the other languages by a certain attribute which Richards had first called "ambiguity." Empson occupied himself with exhibiting the complexities of response which ambiguity engenders in his daringly ingenious study *Seven Types of Ambiguity*. Philip Wheelwright suggests that instead of "ambiguity," the better word would be "plurisignation," which is perhaps a more positive term to suggest the richness of meaning contained within a word.[169]

In *Seven Types of Ambiguity*, Empson attempts to define the "difficulty" in arriving at the meaning of poetry, as "any verbal nuance, however slight, which gives room for alternative reactions," has in it conditions for "ambiguity." This notion helped characterise the terms like "irony," "tension," etc. employed by the New Critics as tools for understanding the complex nature of poetic structure.

Irony, for the New Critics, is a term which brings together the tension between different intellectual or emotional forces existing within a verbal structure. It balances heterogeneous impulses within the text. For Cleanth Brooks, it is a necessary condition of good poetry. The meaning of a poetic statement is "charged" or qualified by the context in which it appears, everything in the poem providing context for every other thing. Brooks calls this mutual constitution irony. In evaluating a poem, then, Richards says, "We are forced to raise the question as to whether the statement grows properly out of a context; whether it is 'ironical'—or merely shallow, glib, sentimental."[170]

Yvor Winters, another critic connected with the New Criticism, distinguishes between the two basic ways in which

169 Philip Wheelwright, *The Burning Fountain* (Bloomington: Indiana UP, 1954), p. 101.

170 I. A. Richards, *The Principles of Literary Criticism* (London: Kegan Paul, 1967), p. 732.

the poet might represent his hero's emotions: by "motivating" the emotion after detailing the events which produced it; by defining the emotion through a symbol or series of analogies. In fact, Winters clearly adapts T. S. Eliot's useful distinction between emotive and objective correlative.

Another critic who has left a distinct impact upon the New Criticism is Kenneth Burke. He is concerned with right meanings. Burke's concept of language as dramatised rhetoric takes him to investigate language, which resulted in strange results harmonizing the sublime with the common place. He has shown the ways the mind works in the written word. He seems to agree with Richards that form is basic to the analysis of poetry and not merely a literary adjunct; information is a means and not an end; science is interested in facts whereas poetry is interested in aesthetic effects. While generally agreeing on the nature of the distinctive properties of literature, Richards and the Formalists differed significantly in deciding on these properties. The Formalists believed that the properties are the inherent characteristics of literature; for Richards these properties are related to the human experience and value. The literary form was not important for Richards; what he was genuinely concerned with was analyzing the process of reading, reader's response to literary texts and evaluating the experience and responses of the readers. Criticism, then, for Richards is finding out: "What gives the experience of reading a certain poem its value ? How is the experience better than another?"[171]

Since art is concerned with the personal and the social aspect of our lives, critics of art/literature should have a theory of communication and theory of valuation. Richards has developed such a theoretical framework. In his *Principles of Literary Criticism* and *The Meaning of Meaning*, Richards has provided a theoretical framework on the function of language.

171 I. A. Richards, *The Principles of Literary Criticism.*, p. 734.

Language, according to him, functions in two different ways. The symbolic or referential function, the best example of which is the scientific texts, addresses the objective world without any display of emotion. The emotive function of language, on the other hand, evokes emotions and feelings through words which we associate with emotions. The emotive function of language is evident in literature, the shorthand of which, is poetry. Poetry, then, Richards says, is a "pseudo-statement" because, in it "the question of belief or disbelief, in the intellectual sense never arises."[172]

Richards feels that while reading poetry we don't usually see the word with the things it represents in an objective sense; poetry leads us intuitively to areas which can only be felt. Poetry is therefore special because it has an aesthetic value brought out by the emotive use of language. In this way, Richards comes closer to the views of the Formalists so far as the aesthetic appeal of poetry is concerned, but he differs from them in his emphasis on the emotive use of language. Jakobson, however, associates the emotive with the "conative," which is different from the poetic use of language. Richards, unlike the Formalists, does not stress the distinction between the poetic and the ordinary discourse. He is more concerned with the difference between the poetic and referential language and stresses the emotive aspect of poetic language which, he says, differs in degree and not in kind from other emotive experiences. He says, "Man is not in any sense primarily an intelligence; he is a system of interests."[173] Our interests and impulses as social beings and as individuals contradict each other. Morality becomes a question of organising these contradictory desires to harmony and satisfaction because goodness, writes Richards, "is the exercise of impulses and

172 I. A. Richards, *Practical Criticism*. (London: Kegan Paul, 1929), p. 277.

173 I. A. Richards, *Science and Poetry*. (London: Kegan Paul, 1926), p. 21.

the satisfaction of their appentencies."[174] "Appentency" is conscious or unconscious desires and these desires, Richards would say, are valuable in the degree in which they tend to reduce waste and frustrations."[175]

What makes the poetic experience different from other emotive experiences is that it organizes and orders contradicting emotions and impulses into a harmonious whole to the highest level. In our everyday life we tend to suppress some of our conflicting feelings, but poetry, Richards suggests, perpetuates "hours in the lives of exceptional people, when their control and command of experience is at its highest."[176] He says again, "Nearly all good poetry is disconcerting."[177] This may sound contradictory, but when we look at these two statements closely we find that Richards comes closer to the Formalist notion of defamiliarization without thinking in terms of the form but with experience because he is basically a humanist with a theory of value which is essentially a materialist one. He tries to see the relevance of poetry in terms of life. Poetry, he writes in *Science and Poetry*, is "capable of saving us."[178] Poetry tells us, "what to feel" and "what to do." Poetry, therefore, becomes a substitute for religion and philosophy.

Richards views the author-text-reader relationship in a broad theoretical framework. He gives a lot of importance to readers because of his strong conviction on *experience* that art produces. The reader has to bring in the "relevant mental condition" corresponding to that of the author while reading a particular text. The activity of the reader and of the critic is then the same. Richards defines a poem as "the experience

---

174 I. A. Richards, *Practical Criticism.*, 44.

175 I. A. Richards, *Practical Criticism;* 45.

176 I. A. Richards, *Practical Criticism*, 22.

177 Richards, *Practical Criticism*, 254.

178 Richards, *Science and Poetry*, 82.

of the right kind a reader has when he peruses the verses."[179] The right kind of reader, according to him, is the one who has the same emotional experience within him as does the poet while writing the poem. As Richards says, the right kind of the reader gathers "the relevant experience of the poet when contemplating the completed composition."[180]

The literary text is simply a medium for conveying the experience of the author to his readers. The readers/critics should approach the text with the right attention. Richards believes that the right attention may be difficult to have, but it is not impossible. Richards' emphasis on the "reader" and the text as a medium for conveying the author's experience to the reader may seem quite old-fashioned in the context of contemporary literary theory's emphasis on the independent existence of the text, but it is not a surprising idea while taking into account the entire context in which this idea is formulated.

It may be mentioned here that Richards' theory of communication has striking parallels with the Indian theory of *Sadharanikarana*. *Sadharanikarana* (transpersonalization) implies that the responsive reader has within him latent impressions of emotions experienced previously. These are known as *Purvavasana* (latent emotions). The *sthayibhavas* (emotions) lie dormant in the form of *vasana* in his memory. When he reads or witnesses a clear representation of appropriate *vibhavas* (determinants), *anubhavas* (physical effects) and *sancaribhavas* (transitory mental state), these latent impressions are evoked and developed to such a pitch that they are realized in their universal form, devoid of personal or individual emotions. In this impersonalized state, the feelings are always pleasurable, and are enjoyed in the form of rasa, through an exuberance of *sattva-guna*.

179 Richards, *Science and Poetry*, 10.

180 Richards, *The Principles of Literary Criticism*, 178.

Eliot was opposed to Richards' view of the emotive function of poetic language. He also dismissed the notion that poetry is a medium of communicating the poet's emotive experience to his readers. According to him, poetry is an escape from personality. "Poetry," he says, "is not a turning loose of emotion but an escape from emotion; it is not the expression of personality, but an escape from personality."[181] It is through the "*objective correlative*," i.e., objectifying feelings and emotion indirectly through the description of things the poetic effect of a work of art is expressed.

The Sanskrit poeticians call this effect *rasa-dhvani; rasa* strikes the readers through the organized and patterned form of the poem. Poetry does not merely express emotions in their rawness. If it were so, a painful experience or tragedy would not have been enjoyed in the theatre. The process which transforms emotions into aesthetic pleasure (rasa) involves universalization and impersonalization.

Eliot admired the poets because they "incorporated their erudition into their sensibility."[182] So unlike Richards, Eliot believes that the experience of the reader and that of the author must be different. He says, "...what a poem means is as much what it means to others as what it means to the author."[183]

Influenced by the humanistic, empiricist and organicist theory of I.A. Richards, the New Criticism began to focus on description and analysis in critical reading. Though quite close to the Formalist thought, the New Criticism seemed more influenced by T. S. Eliot. Eliot's essay "The Tradition and Individual Talent" (1919) breaks a new ground in literary criticism and paves the way for the New Critical emphasis on close reading.

---

181 T. S. Eliot, *The Sacred Wood* (London: Methuen, 1920), pp. 52-3.

182 Eliot, *Selected Essays* (London: Faber and Faber, 1972), p. 286.

183 Eliot, *The Use of Poetry and the Use of Criticism* (London: Faber, 1955), p. 130.

John Crowe Ransom in his book entitled *The New Criticism*, published in 1941, coined the "New Criticism" for literary theory and inaugurated a new trend in critical method. Two of the major writers of the movement, W.K. Wimsatt and Monroe Beardsley, published jointly essays titled "The Intentional Fallacy" and "The Affective Fallacy" in the *Sewanee Review* in 1946 and 1949, respectively, laying foundation for a theoretical basis of criticism dealing with the specifically literary aspects of the text and expounding an alternative to the positivistic and biographical criticism.

Wimsatt and Beardsley argued that a literary text is an object of the public domain and not the private creation of an individual. So the criticism should be concerned with only what the text reveals. The historical context is important only to the extent it is intrinsic to the text. In this aspect theirs are similar to Richards' views regarding the restrictive nature of history. But these two New Critics are against Richards' view of poetry as a means of conveying experience of the author to his readers. They are more interested in studying the object with its features rather than focusing their attention on the effect of the object on the reader. To them, studying the effect of literature on the readers is a subjective thing, it is more important to distinguish between the effect and the "cognitive structure" of the poem. The aim of criticism should, therefore, be the study of meaning which gives it its objectivity.

Wimsatt begins his theory with Richards' principle of reconciling the opposites but moves on to a different direction in which the reconciliation does not take the reader's or author's mind into consideration. This reconciliation takes place within the intrinsic structure of the text. Like Wimsatt, Brooks is concerned with the structure of the poem as poem[184] and the difference between poetic discourse and ordinary

184 Cleanth Brooks, *The Well Wrought Urn* (New York: Harcourt Brace, 1947), p. 108.

discourse in terms of their internal organisation. The poetic discourse, according to him, is coherent, in harmonizing the contradictory impulses, whereas in the ordinary discourse such a process does not occur. As Wimsatt puts it, the objective feature of poetry is characterized by "a wholeness of meaning established through internally differentiated form, the reconciliation of diverse parts."[185] Coherence and complexity, according to Wimsatt, are two distinctive features of the poetic language. The meaning of poetry depends on how best the integration of the whole with its parts, on one hand, and the integration of the different elements of the parts, on the other hand, take place.

The New Critics agreed with the Russian Formalists and the Prague School critics in maintaining an objective perspective in criticism, including the notion of the author and the reader from the text and the importance of structure and inter-relatedness. But the New Critics' notion of structure and inter-relatedness was limited to the meaning only and did not include the various syntactic and semantic levels of the text which the Formalists had taken into consideration. Moreover, the New Critics were not much interested in the Formalist theory of defamiliarization, deviance, etc. considered to be the yardstick for differentiating the poetic discourse from ordinary discourse. For the New Critics, convergence within a text was more important than divergence or deviance from other texts.

Unlike the Formalists, New Critics were not much interested in literary innovation; hence they were not obsessed with the fetishization of the form as such. They were more concerned with the aspect of "meaning," which they had inherited from Richards. But while Richards' approach was materialistic, Wimsatt and Brooks' were mentalistic. Richards had seen meaning in terms of the words evoking feelings. Poetry,

---

185 W. K. Wimsatt, *The Verbal Icon* (New York: University of Kentucky Press, 1954), p. 236.

according to him, does not merely reflect/refer to things; it refers and relates to emotions. Wimsatt and Brooks addressed this issue differently. They agreed that poetic language does not merely refer to things directly like scientific language, but it also does not relate to emotion, it has more to do with knowledge.

According to the New Critics, the characteristic feature of poetry consists in its organization of meaning as belonging to the public domain which the readers sharing the same cultural background can associate with. They emphasized more the public than the private domain of meaning. Wimsatt's and Brooks' idea of meaning seems to be "an uncomfortable mixture" of Richards' and Saussure's definition of meaning. While they agree with Saussure even without having read his work that meaning is a social convention which is arbitrarily fixed, they delimit this notion by relating the meaning to the poem's "reality." In this sense, they are closer to Richards. Coherence or associating meaning with the words of the text can be a mental activity. But ultimately the words are employed to enrich and enhance the reader's perspective and experience of the world. The coherence of literature takes us to the reality of the world. For Wimsatt and Brooks, who are more like Richards, language/structure is not a prison-house, which is a closed system and takes us away from reality, but has a humanizing function. As Wimsatt says, "Poetry is a complex kind of verbal construction in which the dimension of coherence is by various techniques of implication greatly enhanced and thus generates an extra dimension of correspondence to reality, the symbolic or analogical."[186] The relation of art to life and reality is again reinforced in their jointly written *Literary Criticism: A Short History*, in which they say that art "ought to have the concreteness which comes from recognizing reality and including it."[187]

186 W. K. Wimsatt, *The Verbal Icon*, 241.

187 Cleanth Brooks and W. K. Wimsatt, *Literary Criticism: A Short History* (London: Routledge, 1957), p. 743.

Wimsatt's and Brooks' views on poetry can be stated in this way: specific property of poetry is the reconciliation of opposite and conflicting impulses. Poetry harmonizes contradictory impulses by organizing the meanings in a coherent and objective way, which other types of discourse do not succeed in achieving. This organisation makes the poetic language different from other types of languages because of its metaphoricity. Wimsatt emphasizes metaphor because it is in metaphor, as he puts it, that "two clearly and substantially named objects... are brought into such a context that they face each other with fullest relevance and illumination..."[188] In spite of their insistence on "objectivity" of meaning, the New Critics did not look for the denotative meaning. It is only through connotative meanings that, they believed, the complexity of the poem is brought to the fore.

Wimsatt quotes a passage from Donne's "A Valediction: Forbidding Mourning" as an example of metaphor.[189] Though the comparison of the separation of the two lovers and the hammering of gold into a leaf-form is quite distinct, yet a series of connections can be established through this metaphor. Wimsatt believes that such connections are equally valid and justifiable in our real life experiences. As he puts it, "Poetry is that type of verbal structure where truth of reference or correspondence reaches a maximum degree of fusion with truth of coherence–or where external and internal relation have intimately mutual reflections."[190] In fact, Wimsatt believes, not only the isolated images in a poem can be seen as an example of metaphor, but even the whole narrative can act as metaphoric of a psychological process.[191] Wimsatt considers that good poetry is characterized by 'iconic' properties of the verbal

188 Wimsatt, *The Verbal Icon,* 149.

189 Wimsatt, *The Verbal Icon,* 147-8.

190 Wimsatt, *The Verbal Icon,* 14-9.

191 Wimsatt, *The Verbal Icon,* 85-6.

medium. By using the term 'iconic,' which he derives from the semeiotic theory of C.W. Morris, Wimsatt tries to identify the special quality of poetry from the different features of poetic language. Morris talks of two types of the signs, the iconic and the symbolic, and characterizes the iconic sign as "exhibiting in itself the properties of an object."[192]

Pictures or portraits are examples of iconic signs. Symbolic signs, on the other hand, are of purely conventional nature, like words standing for something predictable. For Wimsatt, poetry adds a new dimension to the "iconic or directly imitative powers of language."[193] So a disrupted sequence of words is an iconic representation of a disrupted/disturbed mind or emotional disorder. More significantly, "the metrical, syntactic, phonetic and semantic parallelism in poetic language iconically indicates a connection of meaning between the terms involved."[194] This reinforces the interlacing of disparate elements, creating the desired effect of synthesis.

Irony is an important concept in the New Critical scheme of work. For Wimsatt, irony is a "cognitive principle which shades off through paradox into the general principle of metaphor." [195] Brooks defines it as the "most general term that we have for the kind of qualification which the various elements in a context receive from the 'context'."[196] Thus in both the definitions the term "irony" is used in a broader sense than we usually associate its meaning with. Like Richards, the two critics use the term "irony" to refer to the reconciliation of opposites as part of the harmonizing process.

---

192 C. W. Morris, *Writings on the General Theory of Signs* (The Hague: Mouton, 1971), p. 37.

193 Wimsatt, *The Verbal Icon*, 115.

194 Wimsatt, *The Verbal Icon*, 86.

195 Wimsatt and Brooks, 747.

196 Brooks, *The Well Wrought Urn*, 191.

In such a broad definition, irony can include analogical and even paradoxical relationship; paradox involving conflicting elements in the statement. According to Brooks, irony is "a unification of attitudes into a hierarchy subordinated to a total and governing attitude."[197] The use of irony in its overwhelming sense is a great contribution made by the New Critics for analysing poetry. It is a strategic term to explain that "the capacity of poetry is to resist or elude the attempts to reduce poetry to the form of a conventional prosaic statement." Brooks' essay "The Heresy of the Paraphrase"[198] highlights the problem of reducing poetry to a paraphrase, which is not the proper way of studying poetry as it ignores the ironic/paradoxical potential in the language employed.

I. A. Richards was the first among the modern critics to take a serious view of the use of language in poetry by examining its comprehensiveness. This comprehensiveness includes an interest in the behaviour of language in an aesthetic situation. He discriminates between two uses of language: the language of the propositional discourse; and the language of emotive discourse. He views the poetic language as a vehicle for transferring emotional states from the poet to the reader.

Ransom conceives of poetry as a verbal artifact which is restructured in the syntax of images. In speaking of image as the language of poetry, he frees himself from Richards' conception of poetic language as mere referent, emphasising the cognitive value of figurative language. Here Ransom obviously hints at the element of texture which he believes constitutes the poem's aesthetic aspects. Texture is a pattern of images. Ransom has not, of course, developed a specific concept of the image. But in speaking of the historical order of experience culminating in cognition through images, he at least frees himself from the kind of confusion implied in Eliot's phrase "objective correlative."

197 Brooks, *The Well Wrought Urn*, 189.

198 Brooks, *The Well Wrought Urn*, 176-196.

As Ransom developed as a critic, he enlarged his concept of language in order to come to grips with the complex nature of the poetic act and form. One of the indispensable technical devices in poetry, Ransom says, is the use of "figurative language for its definitive sort of utterance."[199] Among the multitude of such tropes that the poets take recourse to metaphor is the most important one. He continues, "Metaphor is the equation of the human action to that of some natural object; the object really is extraneous to the human action, but it is made to involve in that action any way, which in effect is to humanize."[200]

The image, in addition to involving itself in the reconstitution of experience as metaphor, suggests "that the object is perceptually or physically remarkable, and we had better attend to it."[201] Metaphor is not merely an object of analogy with the sensory perception possible; it is conceived as more than a mere analogy in Ransom's scheme of tropes. The New Critical position pleads for metaphor a status that envisages a complete integration of perception into the object.

I. A. Richards' exalted notion of metaphor challenges the Aristotelian implication that "metaphor is something special and exceptional in the use of language, a deviation from its normal mode of working, instead of the omnipresent principle of all its free action."[202] Richards points out that the "processes of metaphor in language, the exchanges between the meanings of words which we study in explicit verbal metaphors, are super-imposed upon a perceived world which is itself a product of earlier or unwitting metaphor."[203]

---

199 Ransom, *The World's Body* (Baton Rouge: Louisiana StateUP, 1968), pp. 132-33.

200 Ransom, "New Poets and Old Muses," *American Poetry at Mid-Century* (Washington D.C.: Library of Congress, 1958), p. 11.

201 Ransom, The World's Body, 142.

202 I. A. Richards, *The Philosophy of Rhetoric* (London: Oxford UP 1936), p.90.

203 I. A. Richards, *The Philosophy of Rhetoric*, 108-109.

Richards defines metaphor in terms of tenor and vehicle; the tenor is the "underlying idea or principal subject which the vehicle or figure means."[204] The tenor is that which is illuminated; the vehicle is that which illuminates tenor. Tenor is an abstraction while vehicle is concrete in its elucidation. Moreover, in Richards' understanding of the relation between word, concept and thing the concept or "reference" lies between word and thing in a complex cluster of associations. Thus a metaphor is not simply a substitution of words or comparison of qualities but "a borrowing between and intercourse of thoughts, a transaction between contexts."[205]

As an important constitutive element in poetry, metaphor is a manner of speech that entitles the poet to realize the particularity, the contingent aspect, of an experience in terms of an identity between the human perception and the objective reality, by endowing "the natural object with a human sentence."

Metaphor is a middle term between the story at the expanded end and the symbol at the compressed end. In a strict dictionary definition, metaphor is one of the four tropes, the others being synecdoche, metonymy and irony. It is defined as the use of a word or a phrase denoting one kind of object or idea in place of another by way of suggesting a likeness or analogy between them. A metaphor is different from a simile in the sense that a metaphor is a compressed simile. The distinction is not merely fixed in terms of words used but lies in the fact that similes isolate the likeness in virtue of the things compared whereas metaphors are open-ended and depend on the readers for isolating the likeness. Metaphor is like a nucleus to which indeterminate numbers of particles are attached: a tone to which a not quite random series of overtones responded; a sound that echoed from some surfaces but not from others. A metaphor, in this sense, is more

204 I. A. Richards, *The Philosophy of Rhetoric*, 97.

205 I. A. Richards, *The Philosophy of Rhetoric*, 94.

implicit, more multivalent, less selective and less abstract. It awaits the reader's participation for its fulfilment. So it is more philosophical, leisurely, contemplative rather than being related to action.

Poetry works through the unique principle of suggestion, implicit in a metaphor. The importance of suggestion (vyanjana) in poetry has been widely recognized. The aim of poetry is to capture reality, whether metaphysical or empirical, through its semantic multiplicity-in-unity, and also through its various lines of association. In poetic language, the possibilities of the metaphoric use of language are exploited to the maximum. Properly controlled, metaphor achieves its distinctive, unique value in poetry. Richards distinguishes between metaphor as equivalent to language in general and metaphor as defined in a more limited sense. All languages are metaphorical in a broad sense because to speak referentially at all there is the need to "sort."

Metaphor is closely linked with the symbol. The New Critics redefined the symbol and accorded it a major role in poetry. Some regarded the symbol as a strong form of metaphor. Symbolic imagination, they suggested, mediates between the concept and the object and helps in obtaining the fullness of meaning. This faculty therefore is an agent that aids in resolving the antimonies in a poem by bringing the state of tension into a balance. Tate suggests that symbolic imagination is reminiscent of the Coleridgean notion of primary imagination. Roland Bartei has, however, brought out the difference between symbol and metaphor in clear terms: "A symbol expands language by substitution, a metaphor by comparison and interaction. A symbol does not ask a reader to merge two concepts but rather to let one thing suggest another."[206]

206 Roland Bartel, *Metaphors and Symbols: Forays into Language*, (Illinois: National Council of Teachers of English, 1983), p.61.

Paul Ricoeur employs symbol to designate signs, whose intentional texture calls for a reading of another meaning in the first, literal and immediate meaning. The absence of a definite second term tends to produce an element of ambiguity in the symbol which the New Critics have cited as a source of additional richness.

Much of the French New Criticism is symbolist. Roland Barthes pleads for a complete liberty of symbolist interpretation. Edgar Allan Poe drew on Coleridge and seemed very closely to anticipate Baudelaire's views. Baudelaire, Mallarme and Valery all shared their distrust of inspiration and of nature. They preserved the cognitive and magical powers of language which seems to have been completely lost in the avant-grade movements like futurism, surrealism, expressionism, etc.

In relation to the French symbolist poetry and thought, an image with the power of evoking particular emotions, moods, or synaesthetic relations is known as a symbol. It is an image which suggests an indefinite and ambiguous idea or thing. Todorov places all indirect discursive meaning under the term "verbal symbolism." In this sense, all forms of indirection like allegory and tropes are instances of symbolism.

The symbol is usually distinguished both from metaphor and allegory. The distinction between symbolism from allegory is of recent origin. The distinction, says Goethe, is judgmental. He says that "there is a great difference whether the poet seeks the particular for the universal or sees the universal in the particular. Out of the first method arises allegory, where the particular serves only as an example of the universal; the latter procedure, however, is really the nature of poetry; it speaks forth a particular, without thinking of the universal or pointing to it."[207]

---

207 Hazard Adams, *Philosophy of the Literary Symbolic*. (Tallahassee: Florida State UP, 1983), pp. 52-3. Qtd.

In a more restricted sense, symbolism is understood to be a use of signs that points beyond routine or literal senses or meanings. Philip Wheelwright sums up the use of symbol in this sense in *The Burning Fountain*: "...it is enough for our purposes that we understand a symbol as that which means or stands for something more than (not necessarily separate from) itself, which invites consideration rather than over-action, and which characteristically (although not perhaps universally) involves an intention to communicate."[208] An alternative formulation is that of Paul Ricoeur: "I define 'symbol' as any structure of signification in which a direct, primary, literal meaning designates, in addition, another meaning which is indirect, secondary and figurative and which can be apprehended only through the first."[209] Coleridge's division of allegory and symbolism is similar to that of Ricoeur's:

> *Now an Allegory is but a translation of abstract notions into a picture-language which is itself nothing but an abstraction from the objects of the senses... On the other hand, a Symbol... is characterized by a translucence of the Special in the Individual or of the General in the Especial or of the Universal in the General; above all by the translucence of the Eternal through the Temporal. It always partakes of the Reality which it renders intelligible; and while it enunciates the whole, abides itself as a living part in that Unity, of which it is the representative.*[210]

Coleridge, as we know, had influenced the New Critics in many ways. By emphasizing the importance of symbolism, he suggests that the language of poetry is always charged with the force of symbolism. By according the importance of symbol to the text's structure, the New Critics seemed to ignore that the text was a "living tissue" of its manifold contexts. Everything

208 Philip Wheelwright, *The Burning Fountain* (Bloomington : Indiana UP 1954), p.24.

209 Paul Ricoeur, *The Conflict of Interpretations*, D. Ihde Evanston, ed., (Illinois: Northwestern UP 1974), pp. 12-13.

210 Paul Ricoeur, 30.

that went into it—"the mind that composed it, the language that articulated it, the literature that preceded it, the social moment that conditioned it, the generations that had put their mark on it, the minds that received it—was flickering, prismatic, and unstable."[211] This is a major criticism against the New Critical over-indulgence in the text's symbolic structure at the expense of its spatial and temporal contexts.

The analogy between a poem and the growth of a plant is central to the New Critics which was the consequence of Richards' influence. Cleanth Brooks' and R. P. Warren's Introduction to *Understanding Poetry* elucidates this analogy: "The relationship among the elements in a poem is... all important, and it is not a mechanical relationship but one which is far more intimate and fundamental. If we should compare a poem to the make-up of some physical object it ought not to a wall but to something organic like a plant."[212] Wimsatt argues that the organic metaphor is frequently carried too far when it is asserted that everything in a poem is organically related to everything else.

Murray Krieger, while working within the New Critical methodology, underscores the practical difficulties of trying to remain totally within the world of the poem in this way. He observes in his The *New Apologists* that "on the one hand, there is the need to maintain the context as self-contained; that is, the need to keep out any meaning not necessiated by the organic and closed system of mutual interrelations among the terms which make up the context.... On the other hand, however, there is the difficulty–indeed, if language is considered primarily as referential, the impossibility–of consistently maintaining an unqualified organism."[213]

211 Morris Dickstein, "The State of Criticism," *Partisan Review*, 48.1 (1983), p. 12.

212 Cleanth Brooks and Robert Penn Warren, *Understanding Poetry* (New York: Henry Holt, 1938), p. 19.

213 Murray Krieger, *The New Apologists for Poetry* (Minneapolis: Univ. of Minnesota Press, 1956), p. 135.

For all their lip service to a Coleridgean idea of organic form, the practice of the New Critics betrayed surprisingly a mechanical notion of form. Paradox and ambiguity serve not as elements of internal drama, diversity and self-contradiction, but as elements of a transcendental unity, a conservative principle of order, which cannot be explained in terms of organicism.

One of the major weaknesses in modern literary criticism is either to consider poetry as affective in terms of emotions and feelings, or in terms of socio-scientific ideals. Both these approaches are equally reductive and therefore hostile to the very spirit of poetry, which is both formal and affective in a dynamic relationship.

It is apparent that Richards' original interests were aesthetics and psychology; therefore, his most influential contributions to criticism have been attempts to define the validity of literary value-judgments and to assess the reading process itself in the quasi-scientific terms of communication theory. But, as Tate comments, Richards was unduly pre-occupied with "the fallacy of communication." But other critics were following the findings of Freud and Jung to explain the phenomenon of art. Kate Fordon declared in his book *Esthetic* that all aesthetic speculations as a part of advanced psychology proposed a view of art as expression of emotion. The New Critics have revolted against this whole tradition of psychologistic criticism because this tradition has not considered a poem as an autonomous being or a form of verbal reality.

For the New Critics, form is a timeless reality. They not only consider form as the poem's identity, but also think of this identity as possessing a cognitive value distinct from the norms of other kinds of knowledge. Philosophers like John Dewey, while making emphatic assertion about the inseparability of form from content, finally values a poem in terms of non-aesthetic standards. The New Critics, on the other hand, declare that the value of poetry is inherent in its form.

A poem has no ambitions to provide remedies to the human problems. It, as Cleanth Brooks suggests, "diagnoses rather than remedies... a remedy involves an overt action whereas a diagnosis is still close to pure contemplation, which is the proper realm of art."[214] Thus the value of a poem does not lie in its social function but in its self-defining totality.

The notion of structure in Ransom conforms to the New Critical emphasis on the totality as a closure. Ransom uses a number of inter-changeable terms to describe what Tate calls "literal statement" and "intensive meaning." His idea of "structure" suggests that in every poem there is an aspect which can be stated in prose, an element which any prose reader can discover by an immediate paraphrase.[215] Texture, on the other hand, is described variously as increment, superfluity and residue. Texture provides a "private character" to the poem. His notions of *structure* and *texture* are developed in the following statement:

> *A poem is a logical structure having a local texture. These terms have been actually, though not systematically, employed in literary criticism. To my imagination, they are architectural. The walls of my room are obviously structural; the beams and boards have a function; so does the plaster, which is the visible aspect of the final wall. The plaster might have remained naked, aspiring to no characters, and purely functional. But actually it has been painted, receiving colour; or it has been papered, receiving colour and design, though these have no structural value; or perhaps it has been hung with tapestry, or with paintings, for "decoration". The paint, the paper, the tapestry are texture. It is logically unrelated to structure.*[216]

---

214 Cleanth Brooks, "Implications of an Organic Theory of Poetry," *Literature and Belief*, ed., M. H. Abrams (New York: Columbia UP, 1958), p. 75.

215 Ransom, *The Intent of the Critic*, ed. Donald A. Stauffer (Princeton: Princeton UP, 1941), pp. 89, 91.

216 Ransom, *The Intent of the Critic*, 91.

Ransom evidently considers texture as the aesthetic aspect of the poem having no functional role in providing utility or moral principles. But he does not explain satisfactorily how the two elements, structure and texture are integrated into the single unity of a poem. He remarks: "The poem actually continues to contain its ostensible substance which is not fatally diminished from its prose state that is its logical core or paraphrase. The rest of the poem is an *x*, which we are to find."[217] This statement implies that structure and texture are two separable entities, that texture is super-added, "an increment," to the other, the two being "logically unrelated." It is this unresolved dualism in Ransom's concept of poetic form that leads Murray Krieger to conclude that the concept falls short of an organic view of form. Krieger suggests that if the structure is the logical core, it is a pre-determined presence which is given an "increment" or decorated with "logical detail." Ransom seems to ignore the functional role of texture in providing particularity of context and individual significance to an experience.

Ransom was aware of the confusion arising out of his structure-texture formulation of the poetic act and seemed to have realized that the structure-texture confusion was due to the inadequacy of the term "texture" which is a "flat and inadequate figure for the vivid and felt part of the poem which we associate peculiarly with poetic language."[218] Therefore, he chose the term "organism" which he saw as a composite product of three aspects—head, heart and feet. He maintained that the poem is a joint product of three individual languages spoken by three persistent speakers: the head speaking the intellectual language, the heart the affective language and feet the rhythmical language. Correspondingly, the poem consists of intellectual action, affective action and the rhythmic action. The language of affection and the rhythmical language can

217 Ransom, *The Intent of the Critic*, 86.

218 Ransom, "The Concrete Universal: Observations on the Understanding of Poetry," The *Kenyon Review*, 16 (1954), p. 559.

both be seen as a broadening of the concept of texture, while the intellectual language seems to correspond to the idea of structure.

The assumption of the literary critics has traditionally been that the language of poetry is the *language of feeling*, not the language of epistemology. Ransom conceives of texture in terms of the language of feeling which includes the two elements of affection and rhythm. Structure, which seemed passive, implies intellectual action signifying more assertive and positive presence in the poem.

While seeking new forms, the New Criticism elaborated a complete theory of literary ontology which, among other things, views the literary work as being a linguistic construct, using a special language that differentiates it from ordinary and scientific language. This special use has been termed as irony, paradox, texture, etc. The New Critics have sought to explore the literary language in terms of such tropes as ambiguity, paradox, gesture or tension.

Their distinction of poetic language from scientific language is similar to the Indian theory of art which finds the essence of poetic language in *alamkara* (figuration), *dhvani* (suggestion), *rasa* (emotive element), *vakrokti* (obliguity), etc.

The Romantic doctrine of Blake, Coleridge, Poe, Mallarme and Yeats propounding the essence of poetic language in suggestion is similar to the one articulated by the Dhvani theorists. Both had adopted different methodologies but converged on this point. The Dhvani theorists lacked only the concept of the symbol, which is germane to the theory in the West.

6

Conclusion

Our discussion of the Indian and Western poetics in previous chapters brings us to a stage where it is necessary to arrange the tangled threads together and make a few generalizations on the basis of our analysis and findings. We may also here re-state our perspective and show the striking parallels between the two traditions.

This study has been an attempt to understand and analyse the use and implications of poetic language, especially in the Indian and Western critical theories. The analysis of the poetic language of the two traditions is an effort to discover the possible parallels and similarities. From the analysis that has been done in the previous chapters, it is obvious that though there are parallels and similarities, each has been able to maintain its own distinct identity. However, the parallels are so remarkable that one can reasonably assume that the theories of poetic language in the West seem derived for the ones in India or Indian theories seem to be the forerunners of similar theories in the West. But this is in no way to claim the supremacy of the one over the other. Both had their individual importance. The circumstances and the environment of the different ages in which they flourished have had a considerable influence in the shaping of these various theories of language. Each had its own merits and limitations. If the Indian poetics leaned heavily towards attainment of a mental state akin to spiritual bliss, the Western poetics was biased towards an attainment of momentary sensuous pleasure. Language, which was it self treated as the language of gods in Indian poetics was treated like any other medium of expression in Western poetics. The theory of poetry was elaborately discussed in the major works in Indian poetics, in the ancient time, but in the West, the language of poetry received attention only very recently in the twentieth century, and there is no comprehensive analysis of the various factors which went into the making of a good poem. Although there are certain convincing theories in the West, most of them treated the subject in an elementary manner.

The Sanskrit poetics, on the other hand, had the tendency to devote itself almost exclusively to the pleasure of profound philosophical and intellectual thought. It did not explain fully the essential character of the poetic imagination or expression, and this fact was probably responsible for the zeal with which the theorists devoted themselves to the methodological problems involving facts leading to universal categories. Such an investigation has yielded fresh facts. However, there were glaring defects in such an approach. The Sanskrit theorists, as S K. De points out, failed to realize that "each expression is unique and indivisible; that artistic facts in their unified concreteness cannot, like physical facts, be divided and sub-divided; that they cannot, like intellectual facts, be logically formulated into abstract universals.[219] S. K. De further states that the Sanskrit theorists apparently forgot "that a work of art is institution, that institution is individuality, and that individuality never repeats itself nor conforms to a prescribed mould. They believed, thus, not in the unity but in the duality of imagination and expression, thereby splitting up what is organic into mechanic parts."[220] One cannot write by rules, and words as symbols should be treated as living particulars, an integral part of the poet's institution, and not as a recollection of some abstractions.

219 S. K. De, *Sanskrit Poetics as a Study of Aesthetic* (Bombay: Oxford UP, 1963), p. 77-78.

220 S. K. De, 78.

So both the theories, Western and Indian, need to be presented together in some kind of conceptual relationship, each serving as a corrective to the limitations of the other. The limitations of the Indian theory can be made up by strengths of those of the West and vice versa. Such an approach of complementarity is helpful in theorizing the nature of comparative criticism.

Unlike the Western theorists, the Indians developed a theory of poetic ontology quite early but unlike the Western again they did not have a continuity of their theories. After the 16th century, theories in India almost died down and none of the poeticians made any new contribution towards theory building. Modern Indian criticism fell apart from the ancient tradition because they could not find the ancient theories relevant any more. They began to depend more and more on the Western theories. The ancient Indian theories, instead of being used for practical criticism, remained as the relics of the past having no direct implication to reading, writing and teaching of theory. Modern Indian critics did not try to improve upon them so that they become useful tools. On the other hand, the Western criticism continued to flourish. Each new Western theory, developed in opposition to its predecessor, extended the scope of the earlier theories and developed itself in relation to the needs of the time.

The New Critics had argued that the study of literature could also be a "science." But with structuralism and the rise of linguistics as a strong discipline, the emergence of a scientific criticism became possible. With structuralism, the notion that the primary task of criticism was evaluation gave way to a more scientific approach towards the study of literature and its taxonomy. Thus some of the limitations of the New Criticism were corrected by subsequent theories. But one can say that it was the New Critics who paved the way for a scientific approach to literary study through their minute description of things in the text. Brooks's idea that every poetic work has a contextual meaning other than the ordinary, everyday meaning itself reflects this scientific orientation.

The Russian Formalists, like the New Critics, also developed some fascination for a scientific study of literature. But they gave hardly any importance to the contextual meaning. For them, the literary text was an autonomous structure with no meaningful connection to social history. They were considerably influenced by Saussure's concept of *langue* and *parole* distinction and they viewed literary text as a unified, self-contained entity. They believed in the unity of form and content, which was a kind of oversimplification for both semantics and aesthetics. The distinction of form and content would imply that different stylistic choices can communicate the same logical content but have different rhetorical effects. In this book, I have attempted to study the function of language in poetry in the two traditions in order to understand that there is a commonality of interest between diverse traditions, and that a comparative study of such a common ground will yield interesting results for a theorist of literature.

Bibliography

Abhinavagupta. *Abhinavabharati*. Poona: Bhandarkar Oriental Institute, 1956.

Abrams, M H. *Literature and belief*. New York: Columbia University Press, 1958.

—. *The mirror and the lamp: romantic theory and the critical tradition*. New York: Norton, 1958.

Adams, Hazard. *Philosophy of the literary symbolic*. Tallahassee: University presses of Florida, cop., 1983.

Alston, William P. *Philosophy of language*. Englewood Cliffs: N.J : Prentice-Hall, 1964.

Anandavardhana. *Dhvanyaloka*. Varanasi: Kashi Sanskrit Series, 1940.

—. *The Dhvanyaloka of Anandavardhana with the Locana of Abhinavagupta*. Cambridge, Mass.: Harvard University Press, 1990.

Aristotle., and Richard Peter McKeon. *The basic works of Aristotle*. New York: Random House, 1941.

Banerjee, Tutun. *I.A. Richards' contribution to modern criticism*. Osmania University, 1981.

Bann, Stephen, and John E Bowlt. *Russian formalism; a collection of articles and texts in translation*. New York: Barnes & Noble, 1973.

Barber, Charles Laurence. *The flux of language*. London: Gerge Allen & Unwin Ltd., 1965.

Bartel, Roland. *Metaphors and symbols : forays into language*. Urbana, Ill: National Council of Teachers of English, 1983.

Beardsley, Monroe C. *Aesthetics: problems in the philosophy of criticism*. New York: Harcourt, Brace, 1958.

—. *The possibility of criticism*. Detroit: Wayne State University Press, 1970.

Becker, George Joseph. *Documents of modern literary realism*. Princeton: Princeton University Press, 1967.

Bennett, Tony. *Formalism and marxism*. London: Methuen, 1979.

Berman, Art. *From the new criticism to deconstruction : the reception of structuralism and post-structuralism*. Urbana: University of Illinois Press, 1988.

Bhatta, Mukula. *Abhidhavrttimatrka*. Mumbai: Nirnayasagara, 1916.

Bhattacharyya, Sivaprasad. *Studies in Indian poetics*. Calcutta: Firma KLM Pvt. Ltd., 1964.

Bijalwan, C D. *Indian theory of knowledge based upon Jayanta's nyayamanjari*. New Delhi: Heritage Publishers, 1977.

Binyon, Laurence. *Painting in the far east*. New York: Dover, 1959.

Blackmur, R P. *Language as gesture*. New York: Columbia UP, 1954.

Bloom, Harold. *The anxiety of influence; a theory of poetry*. New York: Oxford University Press, 1973.

Bodkin, Maud. *Archetypal patterns in poetry; psychological studies of imagination*. London: Oxford University Press, 1963.

Booth, Wayne C. *The rhetoric of fiction*. Chicago: University of Chicago Press, 1961.

Borklund, Elmer. *Contemporary literary critics*. London: Macmillan, 1982.

Bosanquet, Bernard. *A history of aesthetic*. London: George Allen & Unwin Ltd., 1956.

Boulton, Marjorie. *The anatomy of language, saying what we mean*. London: Routledge & K. Paul, 1960.

Bredin, Hugh. "I.A. Richards and the Philosophy of Practical Criticism." *Philosophy and Literature*. 10.1, April, 1986: 93-97.

Breunis, Andries. "Some Remarks on the Fundamentals of Linguistic Science." *Annals of Bhandarkar Oriental Research Institute*. LXXVIII, 1997: 249-261.

Brooks, Cleanth. *Modern poetry and the tradition*. Chapel Hill: University of North Carolina Press, 1939.

—. *The well wrought urn : studies in the structure of poetry*. New York: Harcourt, Brace and Co., 1947.

—. *Understanding fiction*. New York: Appleton-Century-Crofts, 1943.

Brooks, Cleanth, and Robert Penn Warren. *Understanding poetry*. New York: H. Holt and Co., 1938.

Burke, Kenneth. *Counter-statement*. New York: Harcourt, 1931.

—. *Language as symbolic action : essays on life, literature and method*. Berkeley: University of California Press, 1966.

—. *The philosophy of literary form; studies in symbolic action*. Baton Rouge: Louisiana State University Press, 1941.

Cachter, Othmar. *Hermeneutics and language in Purva Mimamsa : a study in Sabara Bhasya*. Delhi: Motilal Banarsidass, 1983.

Carter, R, and Tzvetan Todorov. *French literary theory today : a reader*. Cambridge: Cambridge university press, 1982.

Casey, John. *The language of criticism*. London: Methuen, 1966.

Cassedy, Steven. *Flight from Eden : the origins of modern literary criticism and theory*. Berkeley: University of California Press, 1990.

Caudhari, Satya Deva. *Glimpses of Indian poetics*. New Delhi: Sahitya Akademi, 2002.

Chakravarti, Prabhat Chandra. *The linguistic speculations of the Hindus*. Calcutta: University of Calcutta, 1933.

Chandra, Naresh. *New criticism : an appraisal*. Delhi: Doaba House, 1979.

Chari, V K. *Sanskrit criticism*. Delhi: Motilal Banarsidass, 1993.

Chari, V.K. "The Indian Theory of Suggestion." *Philosophy East of West* XXVII.3, October 1977: 391-99.

Charlton, W. *Aesthetics*. London: Hutchinson University Library, 1970.

Chatman, Seymour Benjamin, and Samuel R Levin. *Essays on the language of literature*. Boston: Houghton Mifflin, 1967.

Chatterjee, S C. *The nyaya theory of knowledge : a critical study of some problems of logic and metaphysics*. Calcutta: University of Calcutta, 1939.

Chatterji, P C. *Fundamental questions in aesthetics*. Simla: Indian Institute of Advanced Study, 1968.

Chaturvedi, B M. *Some unexplored aspects of the Rasa theory*. Delhi: Vidyanidhi Prakashan, 1996.

Chomsky, Noam. *Reflections on language*. London: Pantheon books, 1977.

Clark, Katerina, and Michael Holquist. *Mikhail Bakhtin*. Cambridge : Mass.: Harvard university press, 1984.

Cluysenaar, Anne. *Introduction to literary stylistics a discussion of dominant structures in verse and prose*. London: Batsford, 1976.

Coleridge, Samuel Taylor. *Biographia literaria; or, Biographical sketches of my literary life and opinions*. London: Dent; New York, Dutton, 1967.

Collier, Gary. *Emotional expression*. Hillsdale, N.J. : L. Erlbaum Associates, 1985.

Collier, Peter, and Helga Geyer-Ryan. *Literary theory today*. Ithaca, N.Y.: Cornell University Press, 1990.

Coomaraswamy, Ananda Kentish. *The dance of Shiva; fourteen Indian essays*. New Delhi: Munshiram Manoharlal Publishers Pvt. Ltd., 1974.

Coward, Harold G. *The sphota theory of language : a philosophical analysis*. Delhi: Motilal Banarsidass, 1980.

Coward, Harold G, and K Kunjunni Raja. *The Encyclopedia of Indian philosophies : the philosophy of the grammarians*. Delhi: Motilal Banarsidass, 1990.

Coward, Harold G. "Speech versus writing in derrida and bhatrhari." *Philosophy East and West* XLI.2, April 1991: 141-162.

Coyle, Martin. *Encyclopedia of Literature and criticism*. London: Routledge, 1990.

Crane, Ronald Salmon. *The language of criticism and the structure of poetry*. Toronto: University of Toronto Press, 1953.

Cuddon, J A. *A dictionary of literary terms and literary theory*. Oxford: Blackwell Publishers, 1998.

Culler, Jonathan. *Structuralist poetics : structuralism, linguistics and the study of literature*. London: Routledge & K. Paul, 1980.

Dani, A.P. and V.M. Madge. *Literary theory and criticism*. Delhi: Pencraft International, 1998.

Datta, Dhirendra Mohan. *The six ways of knowing : a critical study of the Advaita theory of knowledge*. Calcutta: University of Calcutta, 1972.

Davis, Robert Con, and Ronald Schleifer. *Contemporary literary criticism : literary and cultural studies*. New York: Longman, 1994.

De, Sushil Kumar. *History of Sanskrit poetics*. Calcutta: Firma KLM Private Ltd., 1960.

—. *Sanskrit poetics as a study of aesthetic*. Berkeley: University of California Press, 1963.

Derrida, Jacques. *Writing and difference*. Chicago: University of Chicago Press, 1978.

Desai, S K, and G N Devy. *Critical thought : an anthology of 20th century Indian English essays*. New Delhi: Sterling Publishers, 1987.

Deutsch, Eliot. *Studies in comparative aesthetics*. Honolulu: University Press of Hawaii, 1975.

Devasthali, G V. *Mimamsa : the Vakya-sastra of ancient India*. Bombay: Booksllers' Publ. Company, 1959.

Dhayagude, Suresh. *Western and Indian poetics : a comparative study*. Pune: Bhandarkar Oriental Research Institute, 1981.

Dickie, George. *Aesthetics : an introduction*. Indianapolis: Pegasus, 1971.

—. *Art and the aesthetic : an institutional analysis*. Ithaca, N.Y.: Cornell University Press, 1974.

Dickstein, Morris. "The State of Criticism." *Partisan Review*. 48.1, 1983: 9-14.

Dimock, Edward C. *The literatures of India : an introduction*. Chicago: University of Chicago Press, 1974.

Dixon, Peter. *Rhetoric*. London: Methuen, 1971.

Eagleton, Terry. *Literary theory : an introduction*. Oxford: Basil Blackwell, 1983.

Edgerton, F. "Indirect suggestion in poetry: a hindu theory of literary aesthetics." *Proceedings of the American Philosophical Society*. 1936. 700-705.

Eliot, Simon, and W R Owens. *A handbook to literary research*. New York: Routledge in association with the Open University, 1998.

Eliot, T S. *On poetry and poets*. London: Faber and Faber, 1957.

—. *Selected essays*, 1917-1932. London: Faber & Faber, 1951.

—. *The use of poetry and the use of criticism : studies in the relation of criticism to poetry in England*. London: Faber and Faber, 1933.

—. *To criticize the critic and other writings*. London: Faber and Faber, 1965.

Eliot, Thomas S. *The sacred wood : essays on poetry and criticism*. London: Methuen, 1920.

Eliot, Thomas Stearns. *To criticize the critic* . London: Faber and Faber, 1965.

Ellis, John M. *The theory of literary criticism : a logical analysis*. Berkeley: University of California Press, 1974.

Empson, William. *Seven types of ambiguity*. London: Penguin Books, 1947.

—. *The Structure of complex words*. London: Chatto and Windus, 1951.

Englefield, F R H, George Albert Wells, and D R Oppenheimer. *Language : its origin and its relation to thought*. London: Elek for Pemberton Pub., 1977.

Enright, D J, and Ernst De Chickera. *English critical texts : 16th century to 20th century*. London: Oxford University Press, 1942.

Erlich, Victor. *Russian formalism : history, doctrine*. New Haven: Yale University Press, 1981.

Feyerabend, Paul. *Against method : outline of an anarchistic theory of knowledge*. London: Verso, 1978.

Fish, Stanley Eugene. *Is there a text in this class? : The authority of interpretive communities*. Cambridge, Mass.: Harvard University Press, 1980.

—. *Self-consuming artifacts; the experience of seventeenth-century literature*. Berkeley: University of California Press, 1972.

Fokkema, Douwe Wessel, and Elrud Kunne-Ibsch. *Theories of literature in the twentieth century : structuralism, marxism, aesthetics of reception, semiotics*. London: Hurst, 1977.

Forrest-Thomson, Veronica. *Poetic artifice : a theory of twentieth-century poetry*. Manchester: Manchester University Press, 1978.

Foucault, Michel. *The archeology of knowledge*. New York: Harper Torchbook, 1972.

Fowler, Roger. *Essays on style and language; linguistic and critical approaches to literary style*. London: Routledge & K. Paul, 1966.

—. *Essays on style and language; linguistic and critical approaches to literary style*. New York: Humanities Press, 1966.

—. *Linguistic criticism*. Oxford: Oxford University Press, 1986.

—. *The languages of literature: some linguistic contributions to criticism*. London: Routledge and K. Paul, 1971.

Freeman, Donald C. *Linguistics and literary style*. New York: Holt, Rinehart and Winston, 1970.

Fries, Charles C. "Meaning and linguistic analysis." *Language 30*, 1954: 63-67.

Frye, Northrop, Sheridan Warner Baker, and George B Perkins. *The Harper handbook to literature*. New York: Harper & Row, 1985.

Gadamer, Hans-Georg. *Truth and method*. New York: Crossroad, 1982.

Garvin, Paul L. *A Prague school reader on asthetics, literary structure, and style*. Washington: Georgetown University Press, 1964.

Gerow, Edwin. *A glossary of Indian figures of speech*. The Hague: Mouton, 1987.

Ghatage, A.M. "Lexicography and lexicology." *Annals of bhandarkar oriental research institute*. LXXXI, 2000: 227–36.

Ghosh, Ranjan. "Recentering of the poet and postmodern literary theory." *Journal of contemporary thought II*, 2000: 25–38.

Gill, Harjeet Singh. *Structuralism and literary criticism*. Delhi: Bahri Publications, 1979.

Gilpin, Anna. "The text as an ethical being: on responsibility in academic discourse." *Journal of contemporary thought*, 2001: 67-81.

Gnoli, Raniero. *The aesthetic experience according to Abhinavagupta*. Varanasi: The Chowkhamba Sanskrit Series Office, 1968.

Graff, Gerald E. "The later richards and the new criticism." *Criticism*. IX.3, 1967.

Groden, Michael, and Martin Kreiswirth. *The Johns Hopkins guide to literary theory & criticism*. Baltimore: Johns Hopkins University Press, 1994.

Grossvogel, David I. *Limits of the novel: evolutions of a form from Chaucer to Robbe-Grillet*. Ithaca: Cornell University Press, 1971.

Gudmunsen, Chris. *Wittgenstein and Buddhism*. London: Macmillan, 1977.

Habermas, Jyergen. *Theory and practice*. Boston: Beacon Press, 1973.

Halbfass, Wilhelm. "The meaning and pursuit of happiness: Indian and western perspective." *New Quest*. 120, Nov–Dec 1996: 329–38.

Hall, Donald. *Claims for poetry*. Ann Arbor: University of Michigan Press, 1982.

Handy, William J. *A symposium on formalist criticism*. Austin: University of Texas, 1965.

Harris, Wendell V. *Dictionary of concepts in literary criticism and theory*. New York: Greenwood Press, 1992.

Hartman, Geoffrey. *Deconstruction and criticism*. New York: The Seabury Press, 1979.

Hattori, Mari. "On the rhyme (yamaka) in sanskrit poetics." *Annals of bhandarkar oriental research institute* LXXVIII, 1997: 263–274.

Hayward, John. *Points of view*. London: Faber and Faber, 1941.

Heidegger, Martin. *Being and time*. New York : Harper & Row, 1962.

Hillyer, Robert. *In pursuit of poetry*. New York: McGraw-Hill, 1960.

Hiriyanna, Mysore. *Art experience*. Mysore: Kavyalaya Publishers, 1954.

Hirsch, E D. *The aims of interpretation*. Chicago: University of Chicago Press, 1976.

—. *Validity in interpretation*. New Haven: Yale University Press, 1967.

Holland, Norman Norwo. *The dynamics of literary response*. New York: Norton, 1975.

Hollander, John. *Vision and resonance: two senses of poetic form*. New Haven: Yale University Press, 1985.

Holman, Clarence Hugh, and William Harmon. *A handbook to literature: based on the original by William Flint Thrall and Addison Hibbard*. New York: Macmillan, 1986.

Houben, Jan E.M. "Bhartrhari's vakyapadiya and the ancient vrtti (1): the vrtti and vrsabhadeva's paddhati on vakyopadiya 1: 46a atmobhedain/ atmabhedas." *Annals of bhandarkar oriental research institute* LXXVIII, 1997: 176-98.

Howell, Wilbur Samuel. *Poetics, rhetoric, and logic: studies in the basic disciplines of criticism*. Ithaca: Cornell University Press, 1975.

Huparikar, Ganesh Shripad. *The problem of Sanskrit teaching*. Kolhapur: Bharat Book-Stall, 1949.

Hutcheon, Linda. *Formalism and the freudian aesthetic: the example of Charles Mauron*. Cambridge: Cambridge university press, 1984.

Indra, C.T. "The interface between reader–response criticism and new historicism: a case study of milton." *Indian Journal of American Studies 23.1*, 1993: 57-64.

Ingalls, Daniel H H. *An anthology of Sanskrit court poetry*. Cambridge, Mass.: Harvard Univ. Press, 1965.

Iser, Wolfgang. *The implied reader; patterns of communication in prose fiction from Bunyan to Beckett*. Baltimore: Johns Hopkins University Press, 1974.

Jagadisa. *Ṣabdasaktiprakasika*. Benaras: Kashi Sanskrit Series, 1934.

Jagannath, Badrinath Jha and M.M. Jha. *Rasagaṅgadhara*. Varanasi: Chowkhamba Sanskrit Series, 1955.

Jakobson, Roman. *Language and Literature*. Cambridge, Mass: Harvard UP, 1987.

Jancovich, Mark. *The cultural politics of the New Criticism*. Cambridge: Cambridge University Press, 1993.

Jefferson, Ann. "Literariness, dominance and violence in formalist aesthetics." In *Literary Theory Today*, by Peter Collier and Helga Geyar-Ryan, 125-41. Ithaca: Cornell University Press, 1990.

Jefferson, Ann, and David Robey. *Modern literary theory: a comparative introduction*. London: B.T. Batsford, 1982.

Jespersen, Otto. *Language, its nature, development and origin*. London: G. Allen & Unwin, 1959.

—. *The philosophy of grammar*. London: George Allen & Unwin, 1934.

Jha, Bechan. *Concept of poetic blemishes in Sanskrit poetics*. Varanasi: Chowkhamba Sanskrit Series Office, 1965.

Jha, Ganganatha. *Purva-mimamsa in its sources*. Varanasi: Banaras Hindu University, 1964.

—. *The Prabhakara school of purva mimamsa*. Delhi: Motilal Banarsidas, 1978.

Jha, Girish K. "Panini's concept of samanpada." *Annals of bhandarkar oriental research institute* LXXXI, 2000: 245-50.

Johnson, Barbara. *The critical difference: essays in the contemporary rhetoric of reading*. Baltimore: Johns Hopkins University Press, 1980.

Juhl, P D. *Interpretation, an essay in the philosophy of literary criticism*. Princeton, N.J.: Princeton University Press, 1980.

Kane, Panduranga Vamana. *History of Sanskrit poetics*. Delhi: Motilal Banarsidass, 1971.

Kar, Prafulla C. *Critical theory: western and Indian*. Delhi: Pencraft Internat, 1997.

Keith, Arthur Berriedale. *A history of Sanskrit literature*. London: Oxford University Press, 1920.

—. *The Sanskrit drama in its origin, development, theory and practice*. London: Oxford University Press, 1924.

Kenny, Anthony John Patrick. *Wittgenstein*. Harmondsworth: Penguin, 1973.

Khubchandani, Lachman M. "Speech as an Ongoing Activity: Comparing Bhartrhari and Wittgenstein," *Indian Philosophical Quaterly* XXVI.1, January 1999: 1-17.

Kinneavy, James L. *A theory of discourse; the aims of discourse*. Englewood Cliffs, N.J.: Prentice-Hall , 1971.

Krieger, Murray. *Poetic presence and illusion: essays in critical history and theory*. Baltimore: Johns Hopkins University Press, 1979.

—. *The institution of theory*. Baltimore: Johns Hopkins University Press, 1994.

—. *The new apologists for poetry*. Minneapolis: University of Minnesota Press, 1956.

—. *Theory of criticism: a tradition and its system*. Baltimore: Johns Hopkins University Press, 1976.

—. *Words about words about words: theory, criticism, and the literary text*. Baltimore: Johns Hopkins University Press, 1988.

Krishnamacharya, V. *Sphotavada of Nagesabhatta*. Madras: Theosophical Pub. House, 1946.

Krishnamoorthy, K. *Essays in Sanskrit criticism*. Dharwar: Karnatak University, 1964.

—. *Studies in Indian aesthetics and criticism*. Mysore: D.V.K. Murthy, 1979.

—. *The Dhvanyaloka and its critics*. Dharwar: Karnataka University, 1974.

—. *The Dhvanyaloka and its critics*. Mysore: Kavyalaya Publishers, 1968.

Kuhn, Thomas S. *The structure of scientific revolutions*. Chicago: University of Chicago Press, 1970.

Kumar, Pushpendra. *Aesthetics and Sanskrit Literature*. Delhi: Nag Publishers, 1980.

Kunitz, Stanley, and Howard Haycraft. *Twentieth century authors, a biographical dictionary of modern literature*. New York: H.W. Wilson Co., 1942.

Lahiri, P C. *Concepts of riti and guna in Sanskrit poetics in their historical development*. Delhi: V.K. Publishing House, 1987.

Langer, Susanne K. *Problems of art : ten philosophical lectures*. New York: Scribner, 1957.

Langer, Susanne Katherina Knauth. *Feeling and form: a theory of art developed from: philosophy in a new key*. London: Routledge & Kegan Paul, 1952.

Lawn, Christopher. "Gadamer on poetic and everyday language." *Philosophy and literature 25.1*, April 2001: 113-126.

Leitch, Vincent B. "Saving poetry: murray krieger's faith in formalism." *New orleans review 10.1.*, 1983.

Lemon, Lee T, and Marion J Reis. *Russian formalist criticism; four essays*. Lincoln: University of Nebraska Press , 1965.

Lentricchia, Frank. *After the new criticism*. London: Athlone Press, 1980.

Lentricchia, Frank, and Thomas McLaughlin. *Critical terms for literary study*. Chicago: University of Chicago Press, 1995.

Levin, Samuel R. *Linguistic structures in poetry*. The Hague: Mouton, 1962.

—. *The semantics of metaphor*. Baltimore: Johns Hopkins University Press, 1977.

Lucy, Niall. *Postmodern literary theory: an anthology*. Oxford : Blackwell Publishers, 2000.

Mallarme, Stephane, and Bradford Cook. *Selected prose, poems, essays and letters*. Baltimore: Johns Hopkins press, 1956.

Mammata, and Sivaprasad Bhattacharyya. *The Kavyaprakasa of Mammata: with the commentary of Sridhara*. Calcutta: Sanskrit College, 1961.

Mammatacarya, and R C Dwivedi. *The poetic light: Kavyaprakasa of Mammata*. Delhi: Motilal Banarsidass, 1966.

Man, Paul De. *Allegories of reading: figural language in Rousseau, Nietzsche, Rilke, and Proust*. New Haven: Yale University Press, 1979.

Margolis, Joseph. *Art and philosophy*. Atlantic Highlands, N.J.: Humanities Press, 1980.

—. *The language of art and art criticism: analytic questions in aesthetics*. Detroit: Wayne State University Press, 1965.

Marshall, Donald G. *Contemporary critical theory: a selective bibliography*. New York: Modern Language Association of America, 1993.

Masson, J Moussaieff, and M V Patwardhan. *Santarasa and Abhinavagupta's philosophy of aesthetics*. Poona: Bhandarkar Oriental Research Institute, 1969.

Matejka, Ladislav, and Krystyna Pomorska. *Readings in Russian poetics: formalist and structuralist views*. Cambridge: MIT Press, 1971.

Matilal, Bimal Krishna. *Epistemology, logic, and grammar in indian philosophical analysis*. Hague: Mouton, 1971.

—. *Logic, language and reality: an introduction to Indian philosophical studies*. Delhi: Motilal Banarsidass, 1985.

Meyer, Leonard B, and Berel Lang. *The Concept of style*. Philadelphia: University of Pennsylvania Press, 1979.

Mishra, Sadananda. "A critique of the phenomenological attack against new criticism." *Bharati–Utkal University Journal IX.6*, July 1979: 85–96.

Mohan, G B. *The response to poetry; a study in comparative aesthetics*. New Delhi: People's Pub. House , 1968.

Mohanty, Jitendranatn. *Classical Indian philosophy*. New Delhi: Oxford University Press, 2000.

Morris, Charles William. *Writings on the general theory of signs*. The Hague: Mouton, 1971.

Moya, Paula M L, and Michael Roy Hames-Garcia. *Reclaiming identity : realist theory and the predicament of postmodernism*. Berkeley, Calif.: University of California Press, 2000.

Mukherjee, Arundhati. "On creating a poem." *Indian philosophical quarterly. XXVIII.1*, January 2001: 69–79.

Mukherjee, Tutun. "Wittgenstein and deconstruction." *Indian Journal of American Studies 23.1*, 1993: 75–83.

Mukherji, Ramaranjan. *Literary criticism in ancient India*. Calcutta: Sanskrit Pustak Bhandar, 1966.

Munro, Thomas. *Form and style in the arts: an introduction to aesthetic morphology*. Cleveland: Press of Case Western Reserve University, 1970.

—. *Oriental aesthetics*. Cleveland: Press of Western Reserve University, 1965.

Murthy, G.S.S. "Characterizing classical anustup: a study in Sanskrit prosody." *Annals of the bhandarkar oriental research institute. LXXXIV*, 2003: 101-115.

Murty, K Satchidananda. *Philosophy in India: traditions, teaching, and research*. New Delhi: Motilal Banarsidass, 1985.

Muthyala, John S. "Postmodernism and its discontents." *Indian Journal of America Studies*, 1998: 25–29.

Muthyala, John S. "The politics of borrowing theories in postmodern and postcolonial discourse and theory." *Journal of Contemporary Thought*, 1998: 23–40.

Nagendra. *A Dictionary of Sanskrit poetics*. Delhi: B. R. Publishing, 1987.

—. *Emotive basis of literature and other essays*. Delhi: B. R. Publishing Corporation, 1986.

Naik, M K. *Indian response to poetry in English*. Madras: Macmillan, 1970.

Nandi, Tapasvi. "Rasa–Theory: a catholic application." *Annals of the bhandarkar oriental research institute*, 2001: 76-84.

Nayak, G. C. "Nagarjuna, candrakirti, and wittgenstein: a critical evaluation of certain significant aspects." *Annals of bhandarkar oriental research institute* LXXXI, 2000: 123–33.

Nostrand, Albert D Van. *Literary criticism in America*. New York: Liberal Arts Press, 1957.

Ogden, C K. *The meaning of meaning*. London: Routledge and Kegan Paul Ltd., 1946.

Ogden, C K, I A Richards, and James Edward Hathorn Wood. *The foundations of aesthetics*. London: G. Allen and Unwin Ltd., 1922.

Olsen, Stein Haugom. *The structure of literary understanding*. Cambridge: Cambridge University Press, 1978.

Olshewsky, Thomas M. *Problems in the philosophy of language*. New York: Holt, Rinehart and Winston, 1969.

Ortony, Andrew. *Metaphor and thought*. Cambridge: Cambridge University Press, 1979.

Osborne, Harold. *Aesthetics and Criticism*. London: Routledge & Kegan, 1955.

—. *Aesthetics in the modern world*. London: Thames & Hudson, 1968.

Osborne, Harold. "The quality of feeling in art." In *Aesthetics in the modern world*, by Harold Osborne, 105-124. London: Thames and Hudson, 1968.

Pandey, Kanti Chandra. *Comparative aesthetics*. Varanasi: Chowkhamba Sanskrit Series Office, 1959.

Pandeya, Ram Chandra. *The problem of meaning in indian philosophy*. Delhi: Motilal Banarsidass, 1963.

Panneerselvam, S. "Myths as discourse in the structural hermeneutics of levi-strauss." *Indian Philosophical Quarterly. XXVI*, January 1999: 19–28.

Patankar, R.B. "Does the rasa theory make any sense." *Philosophy East and West*. XXX.3, July 1980: 293-303.

Pathak, R.S. "Teaching of language and literature in ancient India." *The ravenshaw Journal of English Studies* X.1–2, Jan–Dec.2000: 1–11.

Pathiaraj, R. "Language philosophy of nyaya school." *Indian Philosophical Quaterly* XXV, 2 April 1998: 205–14.

Patil, Anand. "Beyond modernism: the aesthetics of resistance." *New Quest*, Nov.–Dec.1996: 339–47.

Pepper, Stephen Coburn. The basis of criticism in the arts. Cambridge, Mass.: Harvard university press, 1956.

Perloff, Marjorie. *The poetics of indeterminacy: Rimbaud to Cage*. Princeton, N.J.: Princeton University Press, 1981.

Pitcher, George. *Wittgenstein: the philosophical investigations*. Garden City, N.Y.: Anchor Books, 1966.

Pound, Ezra, and T S Eliot. *Literary essays of Ezra Pound*. New York: New Directions, 1968.

Prakash, K Leela. *Rudrata's Kavyalankara: an estimate*. Delhi: Indu Prakashan, 1999.

Preminger, Alex. *Princeton encyclopedia of poetry and poetics*. London: Macmillan, 1975.

Prunty, Wyatt. *Fallen from the symboled world: precedents for the new formalism*. New York: Oxford University Press, 1990.

Rader, Melvin Miller. *A modern book of esthetics: an anthology*. New York: Holt, Rinehart and Winston, 1979.

Raghavan, V. *Studies on some concepts of the Alamkara sastra*. Madras: Adyar Library and Research Centre, 1973.

—. *The number of Rasa-s*. Madras: The Adyar Library and Research Centre, 1967.

Raghavan, Venkataram. *Bhoja's Sringara prakasa*. Madras: Punarvasu, 1978.

Raj, L. Anthony Savari. "Symbol– experience, metaphorical expression and cultural revelation." *Indian Philosophical Quaterly XXVII No,* Jan–April 2000: 99–104.

Raja, K Kunjunni. *Indian theories of meaning*. Adyar: Adyar Library and Research Centre, 1963.

Rajan, P. K. and Swapna Daniel. "Indian poetics: can it be used for practical criticism ?" *New Quest,* Nov–Dec. 1997: 341–44.

Rajendran, C. "Mahimabhatta on apasabdas." *Annals of bhandarkar oriental research institute LXXVIII,* 1997: 275–79.

Ransom, John Crowe. *Beating the bushes: selected essays, 1941-1970*. New York: New Directions Publ. Co., 1972.

—. *Selected essays of John Crowe Ransom*. Baton Rouge: Louisiana State University Press, 1984.

—. *The new criticism*. Norfolk: New Directions , 1941.

—. *The world's body*. New York: Scribner, 1938.

Rao, B. Damodar. "Relevance of classical western criticism in the formulation of a common Indian poetic." *The literary criterion*. XIX, 1984.

Rao, Veluri Subba. *The philosophy of a sentence and its parts*. New Delhi: Munshiram Manoharlal, 1969.

Raveendra, P.P. "Ideology and the canon : reflections on literary value." *Indian Journal of American Studies*, 1993: 35–39.

Ray, William. *Literary meaning: from phenomenology to deconstruction*. Oxford: Blackwell, 1984.

Rayan, Krishna. *Suggestion and statement in poetry*. London: Athlone Press, 1972.

Reichert, John. *Making sense of literature*. Chicago: University of Chicago Press, 1977.

Reid, Louis Arnaud. *Ways of knowledge and experience*. London: Allen & Unwin, 1961.

Richards, I A. *Coleridge on imagination*. New York: Harcourt, Brace, 1935.

—. *Practical criticism: a study of literary judgment*. London: Kegan Paul, 1929.

—. *Principles of literary criticism*. London: Routledge & Kegan Paul, 1948.

—. *Science and poetry*. London: K. Paul, Trench, Trubner & Co., 1926.

—. *Speculative instruments*. Chicago: University of Chicago Press, 1955.

—. *The philosophy of rhetoric*. London: Oxford University Press, 1936.

Roche, Maurice. *Phenomenology, language and the social sciences*. London: Routledge & Kegan Paul, 1973.

Rodrigues, Valerian. "Facing post– modernism." *Indian Journal of American Studies*, 1993: 7–21.

Rudrabhatta, and Kalpakam Sankaranarayanan. *Rasakalika*. Madras: Adyar Library and Research Centre, 1988.

Ruyyaka. *The Alankarasarvasva*. Bombay: Nirnayasagara Press, 1939.

S.J., Anand Amaladass. *Philosophical implications of dhvani: experience of symbol language in Indian aesthetics*. Vienna: De Nobili Research Library, 1984.

Sacks, Sheldon. *On metaphor*. Chicago: University of Chicago Press, 1979.

Sankaran, A. *Some aspects of literary criticism in Sanskrit, or The theories of rasa and dhvani*. Madras: University of Madras, 1929.

Sankaran, A. *Some concepts of literary criticism in Sanskrit*. New Delhi: Oriental Books Reprint Corp., 1973.

Sanyal, Jharna. "The reader as author: influence of anxiety ?" *Indian Journal of American Studies* 23, 1993: 65–74.

Sastri, Gaurinath. The philosophy of Bhartihari. Delhi: Bharatiya Vidya Prakashan, 1991.

Sastri, Gaurinatha. *The philosophy of word and meaning: some Indian approaches with special reference to the philosophy of Bhartrhari*. Calcutta: Sanskrit College, 1959.

Sastri, S Kuppuswami. *A primer of Indian logic according to Annambhattas' Tarkasamgraha*. Madras: Kuppuswami Sastri Research Institute, 1961.

—. *Highways and byways of literary criticism in Sanskrit*. Madras: Kuppuswami Sastri Research Institute, 1945.

Saxena, Sushil Kumar. *Aesthetical essays: studies in aesthetic theory, Hindustani music, and Kathak dance*. Delhi: Chanakya Publications, 1981.

Scholes, Robert E. *Structuralism in literature; an introduction*. New Haven: Yale University Press, 1974.

Schwah, Gabriele. "The subject genesis, the imaginary and the poetical language." *Diogenes*, 1981: 68–80.

Schwartz, Elias. *The forms of feeling; toward a mimetic theory of literature*. Port Washington: Kennikat Press, 1972.

Searle, John R. *Speech acts: an essays in the philosophy of language*. Cambridge: Cambridge University Press, 1974.

Searle, John R. "Metaphor." In *metaphor and thought*, by Andrew Ortony, 92-123. Cambridge: Cambridge University Press, 1979.

Sebeok, Thomas A. *Style in language*. Cambridge: The Technology Press of Massachusetts Inst. of Technology, 1960.

Selden, Raman, and Peter Widdowson. *A reader's guide to contemporary literary theory*. Kentucky: University Press of Kentucky, 1993.

Seturaman, V S. *Contemporary criticism: an anthology*. Madras: Wasani for Macmillan India Limited, 1989.

Seturaman, V.S. "Literature after theory: a case study." *Indian Journal of American Studies*, 1993: 29–34.

Sharma, Mukunda Madhava. *The dhvani theory in Sanskrit poetics*. Varanasi: Chowkhamba Sanskrit Series Office, 1968.

Shastri, Gaurinath Bhattacharyya. *A study in the dialectics of Sphota*. Delhi: Motilal Banarsidass, 1980.

Simhabhupala, and T Venkatacharya. *The Rasarnavasudhakara*. Madras: Adyar Library and Research Centre, 1979.

Simpson, Lewis P. *The Possibilities of order: cleanth brooks and his work*. Baton Rouge: Louisiana State University Press, 1976.

Sinclair, J. McH. "Taking a poem to pieces." In *linguistics and literary style*, by Donald Freeman. New York: Holt, Rinehart and Winston, 1970.

Smith, Barbara Herrnstein. *Poetic closure: a study of how poems end*. Chicago: University of Chicago Press, 1971.

Sparshott, F E. *The Concept of criticism: an essay*. London: Oxford university press, 1967.

Sparshott, Francis Edward. *The structure of aesthetics*. Toronto: University of Toronto Press, 1963.

Sparshott, Francis. *The Theory of the arts*. Princeton : N.J.: Princeton university press, cop., 1982.

Spencer, John Walter. *Linguistics and style*. London: Oxford University Press, 1964.

Sreekantaiya, T Nanjundaiya, and N Balasubrahmanya. *Indian poetics*. New Delhi: Sahitya Akademi, 2001.

Srinivasan, K S. *The ethos of Indian literature: a study of its romantic tradition*. Delhi: Chanakya Publications, 1985.

Stacy, R H. *Russian literary criticism: a short history*. Syracuse: Syracuse University Press, 1974.

Stallman, Robert Wooster. *Critiques and essays in criticism 1920-1948: representing the achievement of modern British and American critics*. New York: Ronald Press, cop, 1949.

Steinberg, Sigfrid Henry. *Cassell's encyclopaedia of literature: in two volumes*. London: Cassell and Co. Ltd., 1953.

Steiner, P. *Russian formalism: a metapoetics*. Ithaca: Cornell University Press, 1984.

Sutton, Walter. *Modern American criticism*. Englewood Cliffs, N.J.: Prentice-Hall, 1963.

Tate, Allen. *On the Limits of Poetry: Selected Essays, 1928–1948*. New York: Swallow Press, 1948.

—. *The language of poetry*. Princeton: Princeton University Press , 1942.

—. *The man of letters in the modern world*. New York: World Pub. Co., 1955.

Tharakan, Kizhakkethalakkal Mathan. *Western and Eastern poetics*. New Delhi: Prestige, 1998.

Thomas, Paul. *Hindu religion, customs and manners; describing the customs and manners, religious, social and domestic life, arts and sciences of the Hindus*. Bombay: D.B. Taraporevala Sons, 1960.

Tindall, William York. *The literary symbol*. Bloomington: Indiana University Press, 1955.

Todorov, Tzvetan. *Literature and its theorists a personal view of 20. century criticism*. London: Routledge & Kegan Paul , 1984.

Toole, L.M.O and Ann Shukman. "A contextual glossary of formalist terminology." *Russian Poetics in Translation*, 1977: 12-23.

Tormey, Alan. *The concept of expression : a study in philosophical psychology and aesth*. Princeton: Princeton University Press, 1971.

Toulmin, Stephen Edelston. *Human understanding*. Princeton: Princeton University Press, 1972.

Turner, G W. *Stylistics*. Harmondsworth: Penguin, 1975.

Tuve, Rosemond. *Elizabethan and metaphysical imagery: renaissance poetic and twentieth-century critics*. Chicago: The University of Chicago Press, 1961.

Urban, W.M. *Language and eeality*. London: George Allen and Unwin, 1939.

V.M., Bhatt. "Pragmatics of Absolute Locative in Sanskrit." *Annals of Bhandarkar Oriental Research Institute LXXXI*, 2000: 279-82.

Valery, Paul. *The art of poetry*. London: Routledge & Kegan Paul, 1958.

Vatsyayan. *Bharata: the natyasastra*. New Delhi: Sahitya Akademi, 2001.

Vattanky, John. "Is theism central to nyaya ?" *Indian Philosophical Quaterly. XXVII*, 3 October 2000: 411–38.

Vernon, John. *Poetry and the body*. Urbana: University of Illinois Press, 1979.

Vickers, Brian. *Classical rhetoric in English poetry*. London: Macmillan, 1970.

Vijayavardhana, G. *Outlines of Sanskrit poetics*. Varanasi: Chowkhamba Seanskrit series office, 1970.

Wald, Henri. "Structure, structural, structuralism." *Diagones* 66, 1969: 15-24.

Walimbe, Y S. *Abhinavagupta on Indian aesthetics*. Delhi: Ajanta Publications, 1980.

Ward, David. T. S. *Eliot between two worlds*. London: Routledge & Kegan Paul, 1973.

Warder, Anthony Kennedy. *Indian kavya literature. Vol. 1. Literary criticism*. Delhi: Motilal Banarsidass, 1972.

—. *The science of criticism in India*. Madras: Theosophical Pub. House, 1978.

Warren, Austin. *Theory of literature*. New York: Harcourt, Brace, 1949.

Warren, Robert Penn. *Democracy and poetry*. Cambridge, Mass.: Harvard University Press, 1975.

—. *Selected essays*. New York: Random House, 1958.

Webster, Roger. *Studying literary theory: an introduction*. London: E. Arnold, 1990.

Wellek, Rene. *A history of modern criticism/6, American criticism: 1900 - 1950*. New Haven: Yale Univ. Pr., 1986.

—. *Concepts of criticism*. New Haven: Yale University Press, 1963.

—. *The attack on literature and other essays*. Chapel Hill: University of North Carolina Press, 1982.

Wellek, Rene. "The new criticism : pro and contra." *Critical Inquiry*, 1978: 611-644.

Wheelwright, Philip Ellis. *The burning fountain; a study in the language of symbolism*. Bloomington: Indiana University Press, 1954.

Wiener, Philip P. *Dictionary of the history of ideas; studies of selected pivotal ideas*. New York: Scribner, 1973-74.

Wimsatt, William K. *The verbal icon: studies in the meaning of poetry*. New York: University of Kentucky Press, 1954.

Wimsatt, William K, and Cleanth Brooks. *Literary criticism: a short history*. London: Routledge & Kegan Paul, 1957.

Winters, Yvor. *The function of criticism: problems and exercises*. London: Routledge & Kegan Paul, 1962.

Wisemann, F. "Language strata." In *Logic and language*, by A.G.N. Flew. Oxford: Basil Blackwell, 1951.

Wittgenstein, Ludwig. *Philosophical investigations*. Oxford: Blackwell, 1953.

Index